Spa Village

Honouring Healing Traditions

Spa Village

Honouring Healing Traditions

text by
Kim Inglis

photography by
Luca Invernizzi Tettoni

Overleaf: The tranquil confines of Emerald Bay at Pangkor Laut Resort are a wonderful adjunct to the oft-awarded spa. Real wellness benefits can be garnered after a relaxing stay at this world-renowned resort.

Next: Bathing in sarongs is a particularly Asian activity: believed to help purify both internally and externally, water lies at the enlivening heart of the Asian spa.

Published in 2008 by
Talisman Publishing Pte Ltd
52 Genting Lane
Ruby Land Complex 1
#06-05 Singapore 349560
Tel: +65 6749 3551
Fax: +65 6749 3552
Email: customersvc@apdsing.com
www.apdsing.com

Project Coordinator: Chik Lai Ping

The Spa Village brand is developed with a long-term collaboration with Sylvia Sepielli of Sylvia Planning And design (SPAd)

Creative Director: Norreha Sayuti
Designer: Lela A

The techniques outlined in this book are meant for information only, and are not intended to replace diagnosis and treatment by a qualified medical practitioner. The author, photographer and publisher accept no liability with regard to the use of techniques contained herein.

ISBN 978-981-08-0941-6

Printed in Singapore

contents

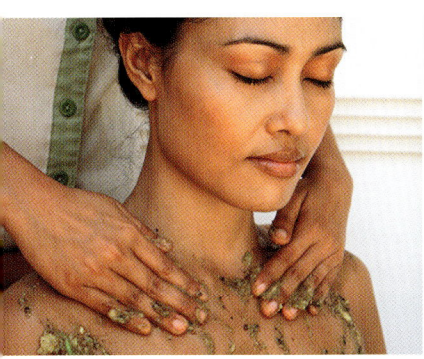

Introduction

Soft cotton beneath, cooling breezes above and the murmur of the waves in the distance. An almost celestial scent of tuberoses. A whiff of crushed cloves and a hint of something spicier. A feeling of deep penetrating warmth spreading through muscles and joints. The gradual release of tension and toxins.
An embrace of wellbeing; healing hands.

Such an experience is only one of many to be had at Spa Village, one of Asia's leading spa companies. Called the *boreh* body scrub, it is a signature treatment at its destination spa in Bali. A potent mix of cloves, ginger, galangal, turmeric and rice, pounded into a mask and applied all over the body, it is followed by a massage and beautifully tropical floral soak. If this doesn't appeal, there's the exotically entitled *ikal ikal* or *campur campur*, a deep tissue, Thai or lympthatic drainage massage, an exfoliation with the island's volcanic black sand, a session of martial art exercise on the beach, a personalised yoga programme – and more.

Alternatively, there are five other locations to choose from. If Bali doesn't fit the bill, Spa Village runs unique spas in a variety of destinations in peninsular Malaysia. Each takes its inspiration from its direct surrounds, and translates the healing rituals of the region into one-of-a-kind spa programmes that nurture mind, body and spirit.

Being massaged, scrubbed, warmed, cooled, pampered and pummeled, cared for and loved into a state of deep contentment is Spa Village's secret weapon.

Page 10: The signature *campur-campur* hot pouch treatment is a firm Spa Village favourite. Combining fresh herbs with heat results in a relaxed mind and a pain-free body.
Right: Malay massage, with its long strokes and deep penetration, is a special at Spa Village. Here, it is given in an outdoor pavilion at Pangkor Laut.

An Inspirational Idea

As the name suggests, Spa Village is a spa brand that offers therapies and rituals that take their inspiration directly from the village. Combining the healing practices of local villages along with the therapeutic properties of their ingredients, it provides an experience that is unusual in today's high-tech world. However, these authentic elements are joined with modern approaches to health and wellbeing, resulting in something simultaneously sophisticated and homespun.

As people turn away from the gold-topped cosmetics jar and the packet of pills to a way of life that is more natural, Spa Village fills a niche. In each and every spa, all the mod-cons are available (well-trained therapists, up-to-date equipment, high hygiene standards, intelligent service) – but they are combined with an ancient approach that has kept local villagers happy and healthy for centuries. Its an inspirational combo of new and old.

It helps that the locations where these spa experiences take place are suitably exotic. Each Spa Village is situated in a unique destination, be it a private island resort, a heritage hotel or a remote hillside retreat, and each spa is beautifully laid out with an emphasis on local décor and decoration. Elegant pavilion-style architecture with carved wood detailing, soft batik sarongs, reflecting pools and ornamental gardens scented with tropical blooms are the order of the day. Yet, each location has its own distinct style.

In this book, we take readers on a journey of discovery of each Spa Village. The geographical locale is explored, the different approaches to healing outlined, and the various and varied spa

A dip in the invigorating Malay circulating bath at Spa Village Pangkor Laut is part of the bath house ritual there. It is offered to clients before every treatment.

menus are dissected in detail. We also provide the historical, sociological and medical background for each and every uplifting spa opportunity that is offered, delving into all the indigenous healing traditions and ingredients.

If all the above hasn't got you excited to learn more, take a trip to one of the destinations instead. For real wellness results, there really isn't anything better.

The Spa Phenomenon

Although the spa phenomenon has been around for decades, even centuries in Europe most specifically, widespread global growth in recent years has surprised even those within the industry. As a result, never before have people had so much choice with regards to health, beauty and leisure. It seems that the spa is now as ubiquitous as the office, the hotel or the restaurant.

In Victorian times in Europe, spas were medicinal establishments that people visited to give their health a boost. "Taking the waters" as a means to rejuvenation or regeneration was a European pastime of the upper and upper middle classes. It had a social element as well, but was primarily aimed towards improved physicality – combating derangements of the nervous disposition, building up strength in the lungs, alleviating muscle disorders and the like.

In other parts of the world, there are some parallels: mineral-rich *onsen* or hot springs in Japan are a case that comes to mind. For centuries, people have been visiting *onsen*, staying at a traditional inn or *ryokan* nearby, for both health and social reasons. In India, too, a stay at an ashram,

The blush rose apple, native to Malaysia, is used in tonics especially for problems with the digestive tract and the liver as it is a diuretic. Local fruits are widely used in Spa Village remedies.

although primarily spiritual, is akin to a stint at a health retreat. With these exceptions, in the past, for the most part, matters of illness, beauty, rejuvenation and wellness were kept in the domain of the home – or possibly the village. This is especially true in Asia where families relied on (and still do rely on) family recipes and the local pharmacopaeia for physical, emotional, spiritual and mental health.

Day-to-day healthcare included the drinking of locally brewed tonics, therapeutic massage (often given to elders by children and vice versa), and freshly picked and pounded pastes and lotions for cuts, sprains and the like. Beauty treatments – hair and skin care, steams and baths – also used fresh, local ingredients, but focused on inner health as well as the outer manifestation. Other specialist rituals were devised for coming-of-age events or the run-up to marriage; these focused on purification on a mental, physical, emotional and spiritual level. In fact, viewing the person as a whole – the holistic approach – is central to the Asian viewpoint of health.

The Market – and Spa Village – Today

As spas have sprung up across Asia, many seeking to replicate some of these traditional village practices in salubrious surrounds, the idea of inner-outer health and beauty has become more widespread. Fueled both by the choice available and a general disenchantment with chemical solutions, such spas have become enormously popular. More and more people are planning their vacations around spas, a fact that would have seemed almost unbelievable a few years ago.

Fruits, berries, seeds, roots, leaves – in fact, every part of a plant – is used in Asian healing. Spa Village is adept at translating these raw ingredients into meaningful, effective spa treatments.

In the same vein, more and more people are eschewing the Western medical approach for the genuine local experience – one that offers indigenous treatments using native health and beauty formulations. If this is accompanied by a connection with local people and their traditions, it's considered even better. The idea of meaningful wellness techniques formulated to counteract the stresses of modern-day life – obesity, stress, environmental toxins – has enormous appeal.

Spa Village has taken this approach to its zenith. Working with local people, combining indigenous knowledge with modern techniques and standards and providing an extremely high level of service are at the heart of its offering. In this book we share with you the Spa Village philosophy, all the while showcasing its unique destinations and imaginative healing treatments.

From the beginning, Spa Village sought the help of local people to fulfill its quest of providing authentic spas and spa treatments. Seeking out a family of Malay healers was the first step in its debut venture: Spa Village Pangkor Laut as an adjunct to the group's highly successful island resort. Its aim of preserving local culture and history, and maintaining a long-term relationship with such healers, continues today. This first family is still formulating rituals and amending and expanding existing treatments many years on.

As the brand expanded, other personnel became involved: a family of tribals, a mystic masseur and a Traditional Chinese Medicine doctor, to name a few. Paying homage to these key personalities and honouring their commitment and knowledge is important to Spa Village; as such, we showcase many of them in our Portrait of a Healer features dotted throughout the book.

Lemongrass and pandanus, two widely used culinary ingredients, are crushed and packed into pouches for the signature Spa Village *campur campur* steamed bundle treatment.

Fresh from the Forest

In addition to promoting local traditions and personnel, Spa Village is fervently enthusiastic about local products. Ninety percent of its spa products are freshly prepared just prior to application, and it has a small selection of oils, soaps, scrubs and more available for retail. For the most part, spa menus optimise the benefits of the region's botanical heritage in signature treatments employing 100 percent natural ingredients; more often than not, they are fresh from the market or forest, or have been carefully stored for full efficacy.

Of course, Asia's traditional medical systems – Ayurveda, Unani, Traditional Chinese Medicine (TCM), Malay and Indonesian herbal healthcare, Japanese Zen Buddhist and Shinto traditions, and more – have utilised the forest apothecary for centuries. With migrations and movements, these herbal combinations and therapies have been shared, adapted and reinvented over generations, so promoting them to a wider audience is a particular passion of Spa Village. Because most are not documented and only kept alive though oral tradition, Spa Village personnel believe that many such formulations would otherwise be lost over time.

It isn't only Spa Village who is aware of the bounty of nature in this respect. Recent research into indigenous Asian plants, flowers, trees and fruits is unearthing scores of healing properties useful for both mental and physical health. And, as people increasingly turn their backs on modern chemical components, products entirely derived from nature take their place.

Left Here, a healing *tuam pasir* treatment takes place on Tanjong Jara beach. The warmth from the pouches allows properties from the herbs to penetrate deeply into muscles and joints.
Overleaf Spa Village Pangkor Laut's long infinity-edge pool, *jamu* bar and generous over-water accommodations make this spa retreat a global favourite amongst serious spa aficionados.

A Unique Offering

Each Spa Village facility works to harness the positive energy of nature with high-touch therapies from the East and merges these elements with modern amenities and knowledge. The guiding philosophy of each treatment is to deliver holistic wellness through the process of interaction between guest and therapist.

Most therapists come from the immediate locality and are used to working with the ingredients they find close to hand. Many have been practising massage from an early age, and have an innate intuition about wellness (and illness). Many believe that the laying of hands on another person is a gift from God, so will often say a short prayer before commencing a treatment. This inherent healing ability is combined with a rigorous, modern training programme to bring out the best in personnel.

The overall aim at each and every spa is the optimisation of body, mind and spirit: whether the experience is geared towards fitness, beauty, rejuvenation, longevity, relaxation and stress reduction – or a combination thereof – is irrelevant. What is important is that Spa Village has fully integrated authentic, indigenous treatments into the modern spa world. And it has done it with huge success: There aren't many places in the world where one can experience a near-transcendental therapeutic massage with a local healer in sybaritic surrounds.

Turn to the various chapters for an overview of the individual spas – and for a full glossary of Spa Village natural products and treatments, see our appendix at the end of the book.

One Island, One Spa

SPA VILLAGE PANGKOR LAUT

Situated in a private beachfront enclave within a private island, Spa Village Pangkor Laut is an innovative entity that combines luxury with health, pampering and beauty treatments. The first of the group's spas, it relies on the natural world – the crepe ginger and herb garden, hot and cold dipping tubs and pools, fish in reflecting ponds, waves on the shore, and herbal steamers and oils – for its existence. With a verdant jungle backdrop and an ocean on its doorstep, it is extraordinarily beautiful.

Although it is part of Pangkor Laut Resort, a holiday destination that combines luxurious pampering with outdoor activities, the spa is a private facility in itself. In addition to the airy reception area and expansive treatment rooms and suites,

there are cosy nap gazebos (semi-open zen dens for lounging), open beachside pavilions, a *jamu* bar or café, reflexology path, beauty salon, boutique, library and 50-m (164-ft) lap pool with loungers. All front pristine, palm-fringed Coral Bay where a beach reserved for spa guests is a haven of seclusion. Malay, Chinese and Indian "Huts" with doctors are on hand, while well-trained therapists cater to every need.

The spa is huge by any standards: almost primal in its jungle setting, yet with carefully landscaped grounds, it is a first in South East Asia. Not only is its offering – dozens of bespoke therapies derived from the region's numerous healing traditions – extremely extensive, its natural setting is unique too.

Left The resort's infinity-edge pool blurs boundaries with an outstanding view over the Straits of Malacca to primary rain forest on opposite Pulau Pangkor.

An afternoon here is quiet and contemplative.
Above All spa therapies, including this facial pouch, rely on the natural world for their ingredients.

MALAY-INSPIRED ARCHITECTURE

For guests who want to totally immerse themselves in the spa life, there are a number of Spa Village accommodations on offer. Built in the style of a traditional Malaysian fishing village, they comprise 22 over-water dark wood villas on stilts. Each has a private verandah and restful interiors that are an opulent mix of hand-spun cottons, wooden detailing, local craftsmanship and supremely comfy beds. They form the ideal base, a stone's throw off shore from the spa, for serious spa afficionados.

Above and right Guest accommodations (*above* at the resort and at *right* at the spa) are almost entirely built from wood, illustrating Pangkor Laut's eco-friendly approach. Soaring sea eagles outside the window and all-natural toiletries inside ensure that nature's bounty is part-and-parcel of the guest experience.

Left Outdoor pursuits in Pangkor Laut's paradisiacal environment complement the spa's healing therapies perfectly. Snorkeling, wake-boarding, water skiing, kayaking and sailing in the pristine waters off the resort may be combined with post-sun soothing at the spa.
Below An alternative for the less sporty is a restful afternoon in a hammock at Emerald Bay. With its whisper-quiet, white-sand environs and gently lapping waves, it's extremely tranquil.

A TROPICAL IDYLLL   Comprising approximately 120 hectares (198 acres), the island in which Spa Village Pangkor Laut is situated has all the trappings of a tropical idyll. Virtually uninhabited until recent times, its development since the resort's first incarnation in the early 1980s has been slow and steady, with preservation of its two-million-year-old forests a strong priority.

In South East Asia, where the rain forests have a biological richness and diversity unequaled by those of the Amazon or Africa, sustainable use of the forests' resources is a high priority. Pangkor Laut Resort takes its environmental credentials seriously: More than 80 percent of the land has been left as it was found, with only jungle trails zag-zagging through the dense vegetation; the use of wood in construction is paramount; and a full-time resident naturalist who is an expert in equatorial flora and fauna is on hand at all times.

Left The secluded, white sandy beach adjacent the spa is reserved for spa guests only. After a light lunch at the *jamu* bar, it is the perfect spot for both digestion and relaxation.

SPLENDID ISOLATION, SYBARITIC SURROUNDS

The spa experience at Spa Village Pangkor Laut is much more than just a spa treatment. Quiet and secluded, the spa has an unparalleled environment in which to shut out worldly concerns and seek inner peace. Its architectural style draws on pan-Asian motifs with Malaysian latticework overhangs, copious water features, open-sided huts and therapy suites, and rooms with bamboo-and-batik interiors. There are eight treatment pavilions, as well as a deluxe Belian pavilion for couples with attendant whirlpool, yoga pavilion, gazebo and steam room.

Once a client is ensconced in a treatment pavilion, the combination of soft music, healing hands and fresh ingredients takes over. If the treatment is taking place in an airy outdoor pavilion, the sounds of waves and birdsong along with fresh sea breezes gently lulls the client into a state of bliss.

Above and opposite top Spa pavilions and public facilities are a mix of roughly-hewn local stone, wood shingle tiles and indoor-outdoor ambience. All are located in a pristine garden setting.

Below The Belian treatment pavilion has space to spare – and plenty of facilities too. **Opposite below** The spa reception is a cool combo of marble, stone, wood and water – vital elements that are conducive to healing.

Asia's healing traditions are honoured at Pangkor Laut with aromatic herbal treatments *de rigeur*.

Above right The ginger family are the undisputed superstars of traditional Malay therapies, but other Asian herbs and spices are regularly used too.
Left The Javanese *lulur* (*middle*), originating in royal palaces as part of wedding preparations, uses turmeric for skin exfoliating and refining. Also helpful for skin, this time skin that has been over exposed to the sun, is the cooling cucumber aloe wrap (*top and bottom*).

FROM FOREST TO SPA   As well as forming a suitably exotic, tropical backdrop to the resort and its beautifully designed, nature-rich Spa Village, the forest is home to many ingredients that are useful for their healing properties. Tongkat Ali (*Eurycoma longifolia*), commonly found near the coast, is widely used in Malaysia for its tonic and aphrodisiac properties. *Piper betel*, all parts of which are used in Ayurvedic and Unani medicine on which Malay healing traditions are based, is found in many places in the forest. Similarly, the glossy *Morinda citrifolia*, whose grenade-shaped fruits are often used in tonics, is ubiquitous throughout the island.

There is something tremendously exciting about receiving spa treatments and tonics that use fresh-from-the-forest ingredients, literally plucked, crushed or pounded minutes before use. At

Left The *lapis-lapis* herbal wrap is a signature Malay treatment. A fresh mixture of lemongrass, ginger, galangal and camphor is applied to the body which is then wrapped in warm sheets. Subsequent sweating leads to internal detoxification as well as relief of any muscle and joint pain.

Spa Village Pangkor Laut, this is the usual *modus operandi*. Taking their cue from villagers, both past and present, who use wholesome, freshly picked botanicals in healthcare, spa personnel rely on a rich repository of market produce.

What cannot be found on the island is ordered and shipped in three times a week from the mainland; then, an hour before the therapist is due to start work, the schedule is checked, and ingredients are selected and prepared. This not only ensures their efficacy with aroma and properties at their maximum, it honours the healing traditions on which the recipes are based. "Nature forms the basis of everything we do at Spa Village," explains the spa manager.

With such stringent quality control, it comes as no surprise to find a spa menu that is probably the most varied and interesting in the whole of Asia. The result of in-depth studies into a variety of Asian medical and healthcare systems, it is absolutely vast. Paying homage to the three major cultures of Malaysia – Malay, Chinese, Indian – it also offers a range of treatments from Japan, Thailand and Indonesia, and even a Hawaiian massage.

Holistic wellness is at the spa's heart with guests being encouraged to try a programme based on one of four umbrella concepts: Rejuvenation and Longevity, Relaxation and Stress Reduction, Detoxification, or Romance. Whichever one you choose, it is highly recommended that you reserve a few hours or, preferably, a full day, to fully savour the facilities. If time is pressing, one of the three-hour packages may work well. Best of all is a week-long Ayurvedic or TCM programme with a doctor monitoring progress throughout (see pages 39 and 48).

Water is a key element in any spa: at Spa Village Pangkor Laut it surrounds the guest in a cool embrace.

Opposite and right "Water, water, everywhere" was a phrase from a T S Eliot poem, but he may as well have been describing today's spa at Pangkor Laut. The sounds of lapping waves, tinkling fountains and water tumbling over the edge of the pool are heard at every juncture.

RITUALS TO RELAXATION   Before every treatment, clients are invited to partake in the specially formulated Bath House Ritual, a seven-pronged celebration of the various bathing traditions found in Asia (see overleaf). A truly inspirational sequence, it helps them mentally unwind and slow down, and also prepares body and mind for the therapy.

And, post treatment, rather than being rushed to the door, guests are encouraged to linger: have some light Japanese food in the *jamu* bar, relax in the library or a nap gazebo with a book, take a dip in the pool, or simply snooze. "It's important to preserve the guest's peace and tranquility within themselves after all the hard work put in by the therapist," explains Spa Division Manager, Chik Lai Ping, "at Spa Village Pangkor Laut, we believe in nurturing clients both *before* and *after* their treatments as well as *during* them."

It's obvious, really, when you think about it. The route to well-being is never a quick fix; it's much better to take one's time to truly unwind. The longterm effects will be that much more powerful.

The Bath House Ritual

In Asia, water lies at the heart of the spa encompassing as it does the mind, the body and the spirit. Bathing traditions are both widespread and deep-seated in the tropical world: For Hindus, bathing has been a holy purification rite for centuries and Muslims, too, use water rituals for both healing and purification. The Japanese have prized hot springs or *onsen* since Shinto times and bathing practices are often found on Buddhist inscriptions such as those dating back to 824 AD at Borobudur. Ayurveda, Unani (Moslem herbal medicine) and Traditional Chinese Medicine advocate the benefits of the steam bath, and many of the region's ceremonies have water as a central tenet.

In homage to these bathing traditions, Spa Village Pangkor Laut offers a complimentary 45-minute Bath House Ritual before every therapy. Given in a specially designed series of secluded pools and pavilions that meander through a lush garden setting, it is designed to set up the mind and body for the treatment to follow. The sequence also epitomises the multi-cultural ethos of the spa.

The ritual begins with a Chinese–inspired treatment that dates back to feudal times. In the evenings, when concubines in the Imperial court unwrapped their bound feet, they had to pound them with wooden mallets to ensure that the blood was still circulating. Somewhat less drastic, but invigorating and vitalising nonetheless, the guest's feet are softened in a floral foot bath, then given a brisk tapping with such a mallet. Reflex points on the soles are conditioned and meridian channels are opened within.

The client then dons a traditional batik sarong and enters the cool "circulating" Malay Bath, a recreation of traditional *kampung* (village)

bathing beneath waterfalls. Standing beneath powerful water jets that pound aqua-pressure on tired neck muscles is refreshing and tension-relieving. It also brings a sense of play into the spa, as anyone who has ever watched a group of Asian children cavorting in a river or lake can testify.

Inhalation therapy is the next step: Guests are invited to breathe deeply from one of four steam boxes that contain different combinations of herbs wrapped in pandan leaves. Inhaling the scents deep into the lungs to calm, uplift, detoxify or de-stress is an experience not to be missed. Those with asthma, respiratory troubles or even simple coughs find this immensely helpful; and, if your lungs are clear, you'll benefit mentally as well.

A sojourn in a stylish Japanese Bath House, complete with *shoji* screens and slate tiles, ensues. Japanese-style exfoliating and cleansing with a hard/soft *goshi-goshi* cloth and signature duneberry soap gets the blood circulation up; this is followed by a dip in a warm, natural rock pool called a *rotenburu*. In Japan, bathers imbibe of sake in such pools; at Spa Village Pangkor Laut, guests are offered digestion-friendly ginger tea as a healthy alternative.

The finale to this unique ritual is the Shanghai scrub: here a therapist gently exfoliates the skin as the guest lies on a marble bed in a private scrub house. In China, this procedure was reserved for male clients only, but at this spa where a spirit of inclusivity permeates throughout, the scrub is offered to one and all.

Left A bespoke footbath pavilion with comfy loungers and hand-crafted foot rests welcomes the guest at the start of the Bath Ritual. **Opposite clockwise from top left** The Malay Bath; herbal steamers; the *rotenburu* pool; the Shanghai suite with its marble bed; the Shanghai scrub; Japanese cleansing with soap and *goshi-goshi* cloth.

A wellspring of inspiration, water is central to Spa Village rituals.
They use this elixir of life for cleansing, steaming, bathing, relaxing.

Left The Malay Bath is situated in a private walled enclosure lined with urns that dispense cold water at jet pressure. Standing beneath these allows the water to hydro-massage the body stimulating blood circulation and conditioning tired muscles.

Above A facial steam imbued with healing herbs gives the complexion an all round boost: the heat opens pores and cleans the face, all the while allowing the herbal properties to penetrate deeply into the epidermis. The lungs benefit naturally, too.

Right The restful confines of the Ayurvedic suite with bamboo blinds filtering light provide privacy and quiet for the nurturing *sirodhara* treatment. Coming from *siro* ("head") and *dhara* ("pouring of herbal liquids on specific body parts") *sirodhara* denotes the continuous pouring of herbal oil over the head and scalp. As it is quite a strong treatment, it is only offered as a daily treatment over a period of a minimum of five days at Spa Village Pangkor Laut.

5,000 YEARS OF INDIAN TRADITION

There simply aren't enough pages in this chapter to do justice to the plethora of spa treatments offered at Spa Village Pangkor Laut, but a brief roundup of what to expect is illuminating, and it gives potential guests an idea of just how comprehensive the menu is.

Ayurveda is currently experiencing a renaissance both in India (where it originated thousands of years ago) and globally as people begin to comprehend its ancient mind/body wellness benefits. It seems to have made the leap from clinic and hospital to spa with surprising ease, but practitioners with integrity are keen to stress that Ayurveda's prescriptions are best received daily for a period of at least two to three weeks.

They add that changes in diet, climate, stress levels, lifestyle habits and more are also necessary for true healing.

The sequestered environs of the spa create an ideal location in which to embark on a programme of Ayurveda. The experience begins with a consultation with a qualified Ayurvedic doctor to assess *dosha* (bodily type), present health status, emotional and mental condition, lifestyle stresses and more. "Because this isn't a clinical environment," explains the resident physician, "the Ayurveda we offer here comprises relaxation and rejuvenation treatments through oil therapy. It doesn't encompass medical treatment per se, but spiritual, physical, mental and emotional goals may be achieved."

Left An Ayurvedic doctor diagnoses and prescribes at a typical consultation. **Above** An Ayurvedic facial refines the skin externally through the application of herbal pastes and facial massage and internally through quiet, meditation and the purging of toxins.

It is recommended that everyone have a massage as part of their daily Ayurvedic ritual.

Left As with other forms of massage in Asia, Ayurvedic massage or *abhyanga* is a therapeutic massage, not a relaxation tool. Its primary aim is to move toxins from the deeper tissues into the gastrointestinal tract where they can be eliminated.
Right The ten main roots (*dashmool*) used in more than half of all Ayurvedic preparations; different medicated powders and oils are prescribed for individual clients.
Far right An Ayurvedic diagram showing the numerous meridian channels within the body.

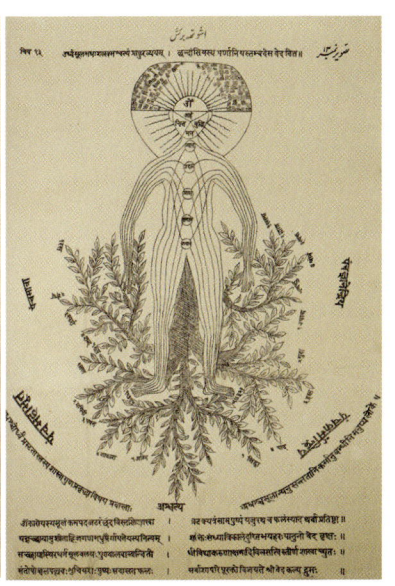

For those who wish to merely dip a toe, or even a foot, into the Ayurvedic menu, the physician may prescribe a detoxifying, cleansing procedure called *dinacharya* ("daily routine"). This begins with brushing the teeth with medicated powder and gargling with medicated oil, then takes in a gently stroking facial massage, the administering of medicated oil drops in nose, ears and eyes, and a head and body massage, before finishing with an application of steamed herbal pouches on the body. "A good all-round introduction to Ayurveda" is the doctor's summary of this therapy – and, since it concentrates on all five senses, it can prove immensely nurturing too.

Other Ayurvedic treatments at Spa Village Pangkor Laut include *sirodhara* and *takradhara*, whereby medicated herbal oil or buttermilk is poured in a continuous stream on to the "third eye" for a balancing effect on the deepest recesses of the brain. In Ayurveda, both are seen as stimulating procedures for the nervous system and are prescribed in a clinical environment for conditions such as insomnia, headache and nervous strain.

Here, it is offered to help the nervous system unwind. Busy brains clear and tired bodies are refreshed. It can also bring deep emotions to the surface, so is ideally only given by an experienced therapist.

All Ayurvedic oils, powders and pastes are 100 percent natural; their primary aim is to detoxify.

There are also a number of Ayurvedic beauty treatments that utilise herbal facial and haircare products from India which are well worth a try. Using such exotic herbs and plants as vetiver, *tulsi* (holy basil), *amla* or Indian gooseberry, and acacia, the hair wash is based on a traditional prescription; since times immemorial, Indians always washed their hair with powder, not shampoo, as powder doesn't strip the hair of its natural oils. As for the *mukha lepam* facial (*mukha* is "face", *lepam* translates as "pack"), it conditions and nourishes skin, opens blocked pores, eliminates toxins and cleanses the face to improve skin texture.

Left According to the World Health Organisation 35,000 to 70,000 plants from global forests have been used for medicinal purposes at one time or another – and certainly the forest at Pangkor Laut is rich in healing botanicals.

Here, planted and wild trees and shrubs shroud the spa.
Opposite An Indian head massage (*champi*), hair cleanse and wrap improves and strengthens hair follicles; it's delightfully self indulgent to boot.

According to Ayurvedic tradition, combining certain therapies with yoga, a healthy diet and plenty of rest can be of enormous benefit. After a few days of an Ayurvedic regime, clients often report improvements in their levels of energy, the condition of their complexions and their sleep patterns. In addition, the immune system strengthens, the nervous system revitalises, impurities are expelled, and there is an increase in the body's *ojas* (the subtle vigour that is the essence of the seven *dhatus* or tissues of the body). At Spa Village Pangkor Laut, experienced yoga teachers tailor sessions to guests' levels of expertise.

Opposite and above In general terms, yoga practice includes the repetition of postures (*asanas*), followed by resting poses, breathing exercises (*pranayama*) and meditation. Here, three practitioners illustrate a series of *asanas* designed to increase flexibility, tone muscles, lubricate joints, massage internal organs, and detoxify the entire body.

Yin is the dark side of the mountain, cool, passive and still.
Yang is the bright side – warm, active and open.

THE CHINESE CONNECTION

Traditional Chinese Medicine (TCM) is another specialty at Spa Village Pangkor Laut, and, as with Ayurveda, it is offered under the guidance of a TCM doctor from China (see overleaf). It also begins with a consultation whereby, through talking, reading the pulse, checking tongue and eyes, looking at the condition of nails, skin and face, the doctor builds up a picture of the client's state of health.

"By listening to the client, asking questions, finding out their lifestyle and their diet, I build up a checklist of dos and don'ts for them," explains the doctor. He also decides which treatments are most beneficial, taking into consideration the needs of the client.

TCM seems to be an incredibly difficult system to explain to non-Chinese speakers, but one thing that becomes apparent after hours of discussion, is that it is a thoroughly modern holistic tradition that has evolved and changed over the centuries. The basic ideas of a restrained life, a healthy flow of *chi* ("vital power" or "inner energy", similar to *prana* in Ayurveda), a harmonious inter-relation between the five elements Fire, Wood, Earth, Metal and Water and their corresponding organs of Heart, Liver, Spleen, Lung and Kidney, and a healthy *yin/yang* balance lies at its heart. However, it is not a static tradition, and as new discoveries come to light, they are incorporated into the system.

Opposite and above The ancient art of body smoking or *gu fang xun shen* includes wafting the entire body with incense, the major ingredient of which is acorus root. This removes all traces of negative energy. As the therapist conducts the ritual, she chants an old Chinese proverb: "We honour the Eastern direction which gives us life; we honour the Southern direction that sparks the fire of creation; we honour the Western direction that directs the movement of life; we honour the Northern direction that protects wisdom. And, finally, we honour your being in the Centre – through this clean body may all goodness come!"

PORTRAIT OF A HEALER: A Herbalist turned Doctor

A passionate advocate of the power of healing herbs, Dr Lee Hui is a 37-year-old Traditional Chinese Medicine doctor from Jilin in north China. As is often the case with such people, the profession runs in the family, with his father-in-law also being a TCM doctor.

Originally employed in one of the many Chinese herbal businesses in his home town, Dr Lee became fascinated with the power of the decoctions, poultices and tonics he was instructed to prepare. Herbology is one of the more important facets of TCM with each herbal prescription a cocktail of many herbs, roots, rhizomes, leaves or more. Each is individually prepared for every particular patient.

As he became adept at the preparation of remedies, Dr Lee became extremely interested in how all-encompassing the Chinese *materia medica* is – and how only a small amendment in a recipe could make all the difference in a patient's recovery, or not. This, and a genuine desire to help people, led to his decision to go back to college to study for his doctor's qualification.

"In China, we have to study for three years, then undertake one and a half years' practical work in a TCM hospital before qualification," explains Dr Lee. He adds that his professor always stressed that a good TCM doctor isn't one that has simply mastered the techniques and the herbal knowledge, it is the person who embraces love and morality in their work. "Compassion is a necessity," he declares, "Emotional commitment is also something we need in our line of work."

This side of the job may be observed in the way Dr Lee deals with his patients now he is the resident TCM doctor at Spa Village Pangkor Laut. A desire to serve, nurture and heal are foremost in this doctor's list of priorities, as evidenced when he conducted a moxabustion session on the back of a young client – movements were quick and efficient, yet gentle and courteous simultaneously.

Preserving health and preventing disease are the two main criteria of TCM, so its many and varied herbal preparations and innumerable exercises and therapies are all geared towards these goals. Prescriptions are both internal and external, with the ultimate aim of furthering longevity and helping with anti-aging. In general, ingredients used in Chinese medical recipes range from herbs to minerals and animal components, and prescriptions tend to be highly individual. All aim to balance *yin* and *yang* and facilitate a free flow of *chi*.

Spa Village Pangkor Laut has a short, but comprehensive, menu of TCM therapies for health and beauty. Some, such as the techniques of cupping or moxabustion and *tui-na an-mo* massage (*tui-na* translates as "pushing and grasping", *an-mo* as "pressing and rubbing"), are administered only by the doctor, while other less invasive treatments are given by specially-trained therapists. These include a traditional technique to rid the body of negative energies (see previous page) and a herbal facial, a bath, and a hand and foot soak.

Tahe roots of Chinese medicine lie in China's religious, philosophical and cultural life.

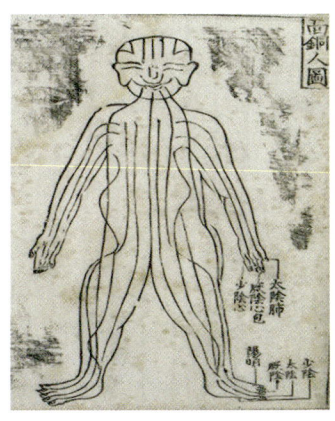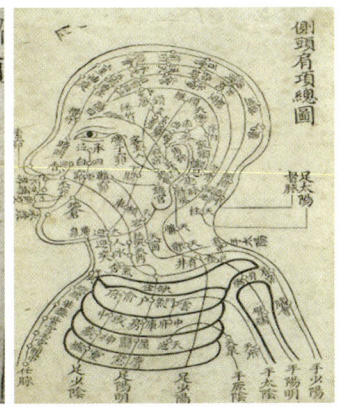

Above Significant numbers of medical texts survive in China, and references to medicine are also found in philosophical works.
Right Spa Village Pangkor Laut's Chinese herbal facial includes a snuff of aromatic herbs to clear the nasal passages, a warm facial wash, exfoliation, massage and a traditional mask of crushed pearls and ginseng.

Chinese exercises are reputed to have been based on the movements of animals.

Left and below Postures, movements and sequences in *tai chi quan* are all geared up to facilitate the movement of energy in the body. Here, two novices are instructed on some basic moves. *Left*, this posture is both a defense movement and, at the same time, an attack back. *Below, from* *left to right*, pulling out energy; two snake heads together; throwing away bad energy; holding a ball of energy; spreading of energy; gold cockeral standing on one foot; a defensive position. **Above** Feet either lead or follow the body postures and movements.

Tai chi quan classes are another highlight at the spa: A therapeutic and preventative exercise, this comprises a series of breathing, postural and moving exercises that have been designed to develop inner stamina and circulate energy. Given in a secluded pavilion overlooking the ocean and the rural island of Pangkor beyond, they are uplifting and energising in the early morning. Alternatively, a private session on the beach at sunset becomes a sure-fire route to inner tranquility.

Herbalism lies at the heart of traditional Malay healing with all manner of leaves, roots, rhizomes and spices utilised.

Left Ingredients for the *rawatan ikal-ikal*, a hair and scalp treatment that uses a paste made from hibiscus and betel leaves.
Right A therapist instructs a client on the benefit of Malay herbs, pastes and preparations, a selection of which are featured below.

THE MALAY MATERIA MEDICA

The third discipline that is central to Spa Village Pangkor Laut is the integration of Malay herbal healing traditions into many spa treatments. As with Ayurveda, Unani and TCM (many elements of which have influenced Malay healers dating back to the times of the Malacca Sultanate from 1400 to 1526 AD), the central tenet is a belief in the self-healing powers of the body. Advocating the maintenance of balance in mind, body, spirit and soul specifically via the four elements of Earth, Water, Fire and Wind, therapies delve deep into the country's botanical resources for ingredients and borrow freely from Arab, Indian and Chinese practices. The result is a highly potent system of therapeutic herbalism.

Based on humoural theory, it postulates that each individual is made up of four elements – blood, phlegm, black bile and yellow bile – the properties of which are hot and moist, cold and moist, hot and dry, and cold and dry respectively. If there is too much of one, and not enough of another, remedies in the form of herbs, spells, incantations, diet, therapies or more may be given. In some cases, such remedies were closely guarded by local healers known as *bomoh* or *pawang*. Depending on their skills, these were (and are) medicine-men, priest-physicians, surgeons, bone-setters, exorcists or a combination of the above. In other cases, though, certain recipes were kept within families and handed down through the generations.

Others have entered the public domain and most Malaysians (especially those from the countryside) are well versed in the properties of common herbs and plants. For example, the betel quid chewed by many contains betel (warming, moist and rejuvenating); *chunan* or lime (cool and dry); *pinang* or areca nut (warm and detoxifying); and *gambir* or gambier which is

Natural ingredients – coconut, mud, yoghurt and more – are used at Spa Village to purify, pamper, cleanse and rejuvenate.

warm and dry. Many Malaysians will know about this and take the stimulant/digestive at different times for different reasons.

Over the centuries, such knowledge has been put to good use in the formulation of a number of at-home therapies routinely used within families for common ailments. Many of these are offered at Spa Village Pangkor Laut, either in adapted or original form – for healing, for relaxation, for rejuvenation and vitalisation, or simply to give guests an introduction to the country's rich heritage and traditions.

One of the highlights for couples is the recreation of some of the preparations for a Malay wedding ceremony. In Malaysia, brides and grooms undergo days of spiritual, physical and mental preparation for their big day; in many ways the rituals they undertake are symbolic of leaving the past behind and entering the future. Skin is buffed and moisturised; hair is treated with coconut oil, rice paddy stalks and pandanus leaves;

and scented baths and steams further detoxify and pamper. Special ceremonies are held with particular foods and tonics, and the couple are counseled on what to expect from married life. At the spa, a series of body treatments based on these traditional practices includes a massage, hair crème treatment, scrub, bath and steam to give couples a rewarding journey.

As if this were not enough, Spa Village therapists are also adept at a thorough selection of massage techniques: Thai, Hawaiian *lomi-lomi*, Japanese *shiatsu*, Swedish, Balinese and hot stone. In addition, such Asian staples as the Javanese *lulur*, an exfoliating scrub formulated in the Majapahit court for new brides, a variety of herbal facials and hair treatments, and a number of warming wraps and masques are offered.

If all this sounds somewhat overwhelming, spa therapists, doctors and receptionists are always at hand to advise, as well as administer. You couldn't be in better hands.

Above Coconut, used to condition the hair, is here mixed with moisturising yoghurt, for a sweet-scented hair crème.
Right Mineral-rich mud purifies skin in the Moor Mud Wrap.
Opposite A meditative moment in an open-sided jungle pavilion.
Overleaf Local materials predominate at the spa.

Metropolitan Magic

SPA VILLAGE KUALA LUMPUR

In the same way that Malaysia's metropolitan city is a mixture of cultures and ethnicities, the new and the old, Spa Village Kuala Lumpur offers a broad spectrum of therapies and practices – from the highly sophisticated to the lowly homespun. Many say that East meets West in the crossroads that is KL; certainly, the same may be said for this particular spa.

Treatments here are anchored in the cultural diversity and rich healing heritage of the Nusantara region. Nusantara roughly translates as South East Asia, so there's an inclusiveness to this spa's offering that isn't found at some other Spa Villages: Most of today's South East Asian populations trace their origins back to Austronesian seafarers who originated in China some 5,000 years ago, from where they spread southwards and eastwards, then onwards through Indonesia to the Pacific. Merging with, and adapting to, cultures they met on the way, they developed into an incredibly diverse body of peoples.

This diversity is celebrated at Spa Village Kuala Lumpur with a menu that includes Malay, Peranakan (a mix of Chinese and Malay), Western and some sophisticated duos that combine oriental roots with modern technology. Examples of the latter include the Trade Winds ritual and the one-of-a-kind Sensory Exploration (see pages 68 and 69). Both take elements of Western techniques (aromatherapy and Swedish massage, for example) and combine them with Asian ingredients and disciplines.

Left Kuala Lumpur is a hectic place, so the spa's leafy rooftop pool is the perfect spot to cool down, recharge batteries and rest between treatments.

Above The unusual Sensory Experience involves the touching and tasting of key ingredients – salt, dates, bitter gourd and lemon – for heightened awareness.

Preserving health and preventing disease are the two main
concerns of TCM: all therapies are geared towards these goals.

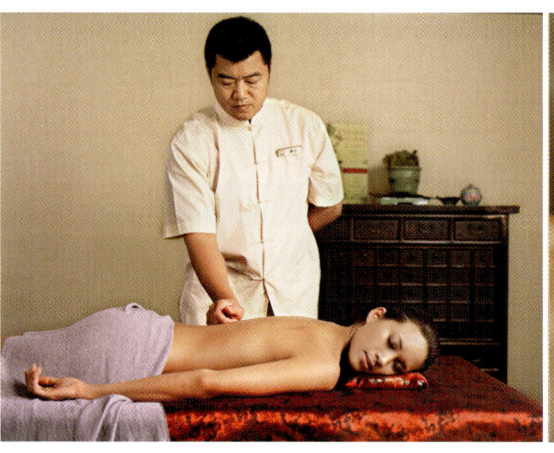
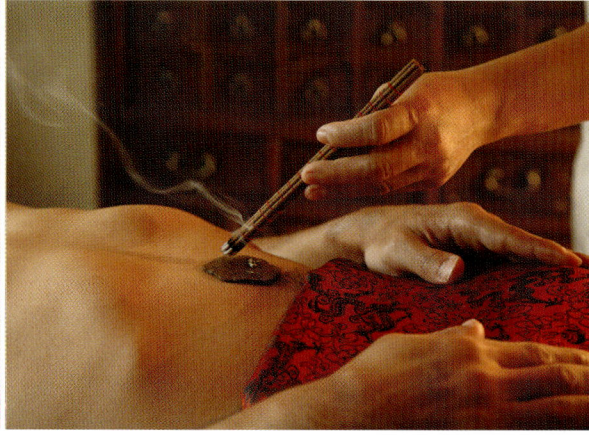

Far left A TCM doctor prepares himself for work. **Left** burning of moxa or the *Artemisia vulgaris* herb – in the form of cones, pastes or sticks placed on or above the body – is an ancient Chinese warming treatment. The herb is believed to be pure *yang* in nature and therefore suitable for patients with cold or dampness. At the spa a moxa naval activation eases digestion and jetlag and improves metabolism.

CHINESE INFLUENCE: HISTORY IN THE SPA

In 1857 Kuala Lumpur was founded by Chinese settlers as a tin-mining camp, so it isn't surprising to find that about 27 percent of Malaysia's population is ethnically Chinese. The Chinese have always been extremely influential in the country, both during British rule and after independence in 1957, so we find many Chinese customs both in Kuala Lumpur and elsewhere in Malaysia.

Lee Jok-Keng, an expert on TCM (see page 121), reminisces about a childhood that revolved around Chinese home remedies. He recalls his grandmother soaking rice grains overnight, then using the water to wash her face "to clean it well and make it white"; she would then dry the rice in the sun and pound it to a powder with green mung beans: these were used to alleviate any itchiness or spots on the back. He also remembers his sister having her face and body rubbed with hard-boiled eggs to

reduce fever, while the remedy for sore eyes was a rinse with Chinese tea. "If it didn't get better after a day, I would rush to the medical hall and get a piece of rehmannia root to soak with Chinese tea again, then we would patch them on the eyes until the irritation subsided," he says.

He explains that the number of recipes in the home is too long to list, but another common prescription for migraine attack was blue-shelled duck eggs boiled with cnidium root. The latter is now known as an effective blood regulator, often used to relieve headache and pain.

Using these recipes from his family, and mixing them with his knowledge of Traditional Chinese Medicine, enabled Jok-Keng to formulate an unusual ritual at Spa Village Kuala Lumpur. Called the Chinese Peranakan Treatment, as it also includes elements of Malay healing, it comprises a number of stages: a sensual milk

Above The Chinese Peranakan Treatment at Spa Village Kuala Lumpur includes a number of facial treatments: resting the eyes beneath warmed mulberry leaves; egg undulation; and the use of the traditional jade roller to cool and relax facial muscles. Mulberry leaves are used in TCM to dispel wind and heat, and are used medicinally to clear the liver and brighten the eyes. Beautiful cooled jade rollers, gently rolled over the skin, help to lift and tone facial muscles, while undulation of hard-boiled eggs over the complexion is believed to prevent breakouts.

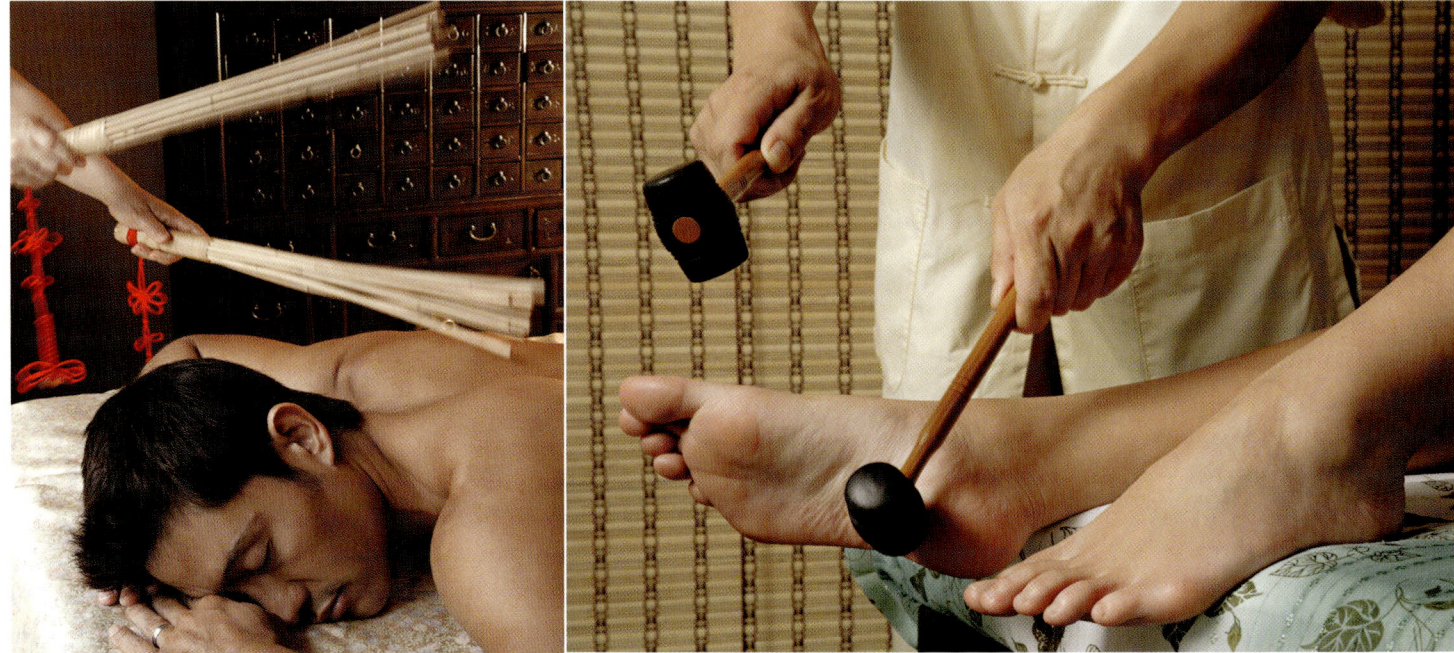

Above left This 1500-year-old treatment originated in the countryside in China and was called *tiao da fa*. It began by using branches from trees, but today rattan sticks are favoured. *Tiao* translates as "branches of tree", *da* is "beat" and *fa* means "method". It is believed to disperse wind and cold in the body, all the while helping to boost both metabolism and circulation of the blood.

Above right Pounding the feet with wooden mallets is another Chinese therapy used to promote healthy blood circulation. It was formulated for women with bound feet.

and sandalwood bath to calm nerves, lower blood pressure and beautify the body; a pearl and rice facial, utilizing the crushed rice from his grandmother's recipe and pearl powder, immortalized by Chinese empresses in the Imperial courts; a traditional egg undulation; and a mulberry leaf eye treatment. Mulberry leaves, mixed with liquorice and green tea and pressed on the eyes, are an age-old Chinese recipe for eye soreness and irritation.

The finale is a full body massage, given first with two bundles of rattan lightly tapped in a rhythmic movement along the meridian lines and, after, a traditional *tui-na* massage. The focus here is on the unblocking of channels, in order to allow *chi* to travel freely through the meridians and ease the digestive tract. As suggested by the name, pushing with palms (*tui*) and pinching with thumbs (*na*) are the two main techniques – both help to release excess wind and cold from within the body.

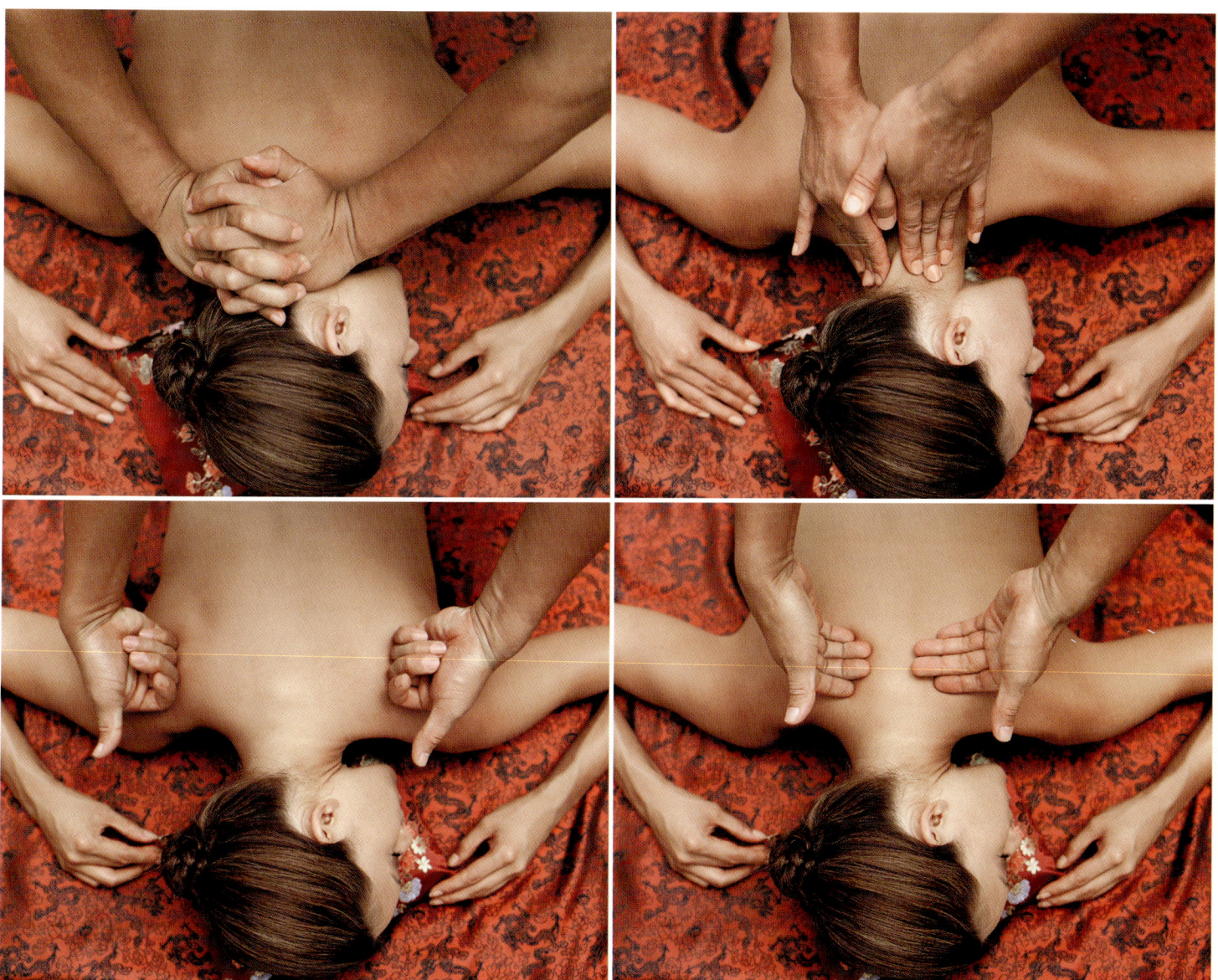

Above Often given to a client wearing loose pants, or straight on the skin (as here), *tui na* massage is a special at Spa Village Kuala Lumpur. There are eight fundamental techniques in Chinese massage, from which all methods derive. They are *tui* (pushing), *na* (grasping), *an* (pressing or pushing downwards), *mo* (rubbing), *gun* (rolling like waves), *qian* (pulling), *da* (beating) and *dong* (moving). As the name suggests, this type mainly employs pressure via pushing and pinching; the focus is on unblocking channels, to encourage *chi* to travel freely through the meridians.

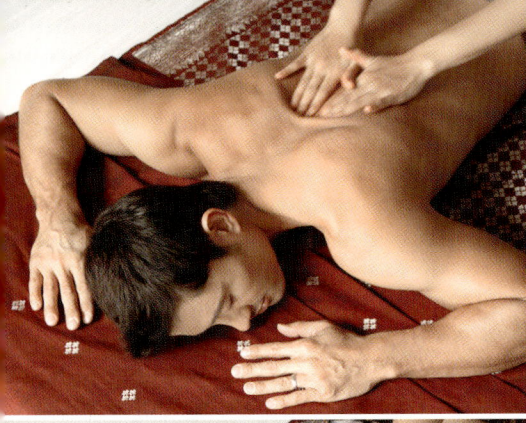

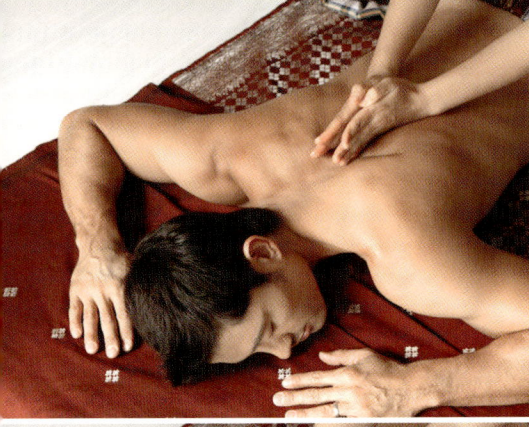

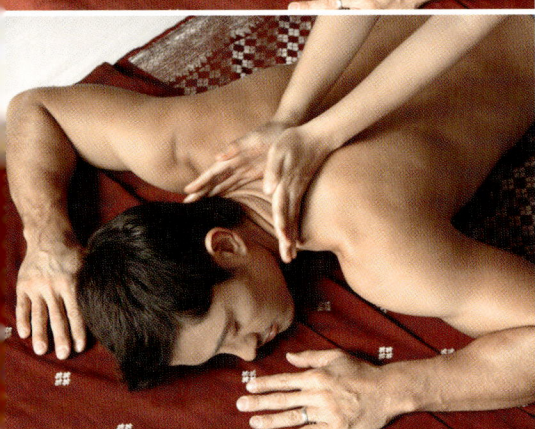

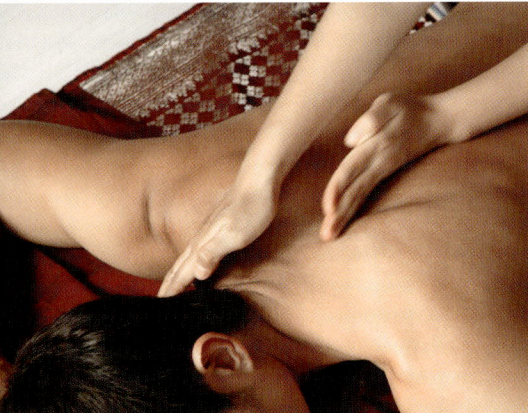

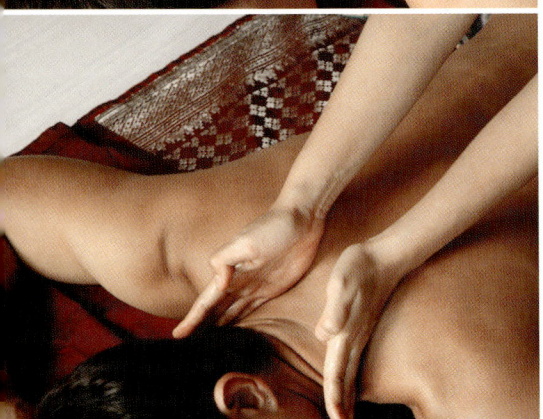

The Royal Malay Treatment gives couples a half day of blissful relaxation – pure indulgence.

Left and above The *urutan pasak bumi* or traditional warrior massage uses some *silat* hand postures in the massage. The oil is based on a formulation created by Hang Tuah's spiritual guru: using blended coconut water and flesh brewed for seven days together with rare *gaharu*, a wood musk found embedded in dead tree trunks (believed to be guarded by wood spirits), it is a deep red colour.

MALAY HEALING, HERBAL BLISS   Over the centuries, the Malay people developed a sophisticated tradition of herbal healing that took influences from Indian and Arab practices (Ayurveda and Unani) and combined these with their native rich pharmacopaeia. Predominantly herbal, they included special steams, massages, scrubs and more. Treatments for men were designed to increase virility and valour, while those for women were intended to improve fertility and beauty.

Many recipes were family based and were handed down from generation to generation with adaptations as necessary. Others were kept in the domain of special healers or *bomoh*, who would be consulted in cases of grave illness or occupation

Left While gents are experiencing the warrior massage, ladies receive an ancient Malay therapeutic massage technique known as *urutan kebaya* that is thought to have been invented by Tun Teja's personal beauty consultant. Renowned for her anti-aging formulations, she used an oil based on the jungle flower known as *melati* mixed with a rare wood musk essence.

by evil spirits. At Spa Village Kuala Lumpur, a family who have cherished their own special remedies for centuries has developed an indulgent couples' ritual using herbs and practices hitherto kept in the family domain. Called the Traditional Royal Malay Treatment, it is the type of ritual that would have been given to royalty in the Sultan of Malacca's court.

As such, it pays homage to the 15th-century Malay admiral of war, Hang Tuah, and the much-loved last queen of the Malacca Sultanate, Tun Teja. Hang Tuah was known for his mastery of the martial art of *silat*, so the massage that starts the men's ritual employs superficial stroking and pressing methods involving the edge of the palm, arm and elbow; these mimic the preliminary

moves of *silat* and are designed to alleviate body soreness and soothe muscle stiffness, thereby improving the body's stamina, strength and virility. The lady's massage, on the other hand, is given with a sweetly-scented oil called *minyak kebaya*: this takes *melati*, a potent jungle flower, as its main ingredient. The massage technique is relaxing, all the while improving blood circulation and alleviating tension and muscle pain.

After these preliminary massages, the couple are treated with scrubs, hair crème treatments, a herbal bath in a tropical garden, facials and a scented body steaming. Anti-aging steams are integral to Malay healing: they expel excess water, wind and toxins that contribute to water retention and lethargy.

Left above Part of the rose therapy, the hair wrap contains jojoba to regulate oil and remove sebum from the scalp, rose to de-stress, grape to refresh and geranium to balance.
Left below Ingredients used in the gentlemen's *gandapura* scrub (top centre) include camphor, lime, soya bean, rice, lemongrass and papaya.

Below After receiving the rose petal body masque, which consists of rose petals for de-stressing, rice powder for exfoliation and toning, and soya oil, rich in vitamin E, to nourish the skin, guests are invited to sit in a steam room to allow the ingredients to be fully absorbed. Jasmine blooms are sometimes added to boost the scent.

The herbal properties are then more easily assimilated into the body – leaving skin smooth, clean and taut. The finale of the ritual involves sipping herbal tea and indulging in a specially concocted herbal remedy wrapped in betel leaf, traditionally chewed to restore strength and delay aging.

Two other signature treatments, based on the plants, flora and herbs of South East Asia complete the Nusantara menu. The *gandapura* (gentleman's) treatment utilises papaya and steam, while ladies can opt for the rose therapy whereby lavender and rose are used for fragrant effect. After a hair treatment, a rose petal body masque is applied and left on while relaxing in the steam room. This is followed by a milk bath and full body massage.

Portrait of a Healer: A Keeper (and Sharer) of Herbal Secrets

The inspiration, mentor and recipe formulator for many of the traditional Malay treatments in the various Spa Village venues, Datin Sharifah Anisah Barakbah comes from a family rich in healing traditions. As a child she used to assist her grandmother to formulate herbal pastes, scrubs, elixirs and more and watched her as she practised various treatments on friends and family. Later, as an adult, she began doing the same and then went on to start her own company manufacturing and selling these 100 percent natural herbal remedies in the form of pills, potions and other products.

The recipes that she inherited from her family have a history that goes back 800 years. Family records indicate that there are three main sources for these formulations: Hadramaut in Yemen, the *kraton* (court) in Solo, central Java, and Siak, Jambi annd Palembang in Sumatra. It's known that around 1900, groups of families from these three locations migrated to peninsular Malaysia, and subsequently inter-married and pooled their ancient family formulas.

Datin Sharifah Anisah Barakbah is well known in Malaysia for her products that trade under the brand name of Nona Roguy. The trend in the 1990s towards more natural solutions to health and beauty benefited her company, so it wasn't surprising that she was invited to help set up the Malay spa menu when Spa Village was conceptualized in 2002.

Left Datin Sharifah Anisah Barakbah combines her own herbal knowledge with new discoveries at her company's science and technology department. **Below** Ingredients for the Datin's *ukup kering* or dry herbal steam, used by Malay women after menstruation and/or birth confinement to promote feminine hygiene. Freshly pounded turmeric, black seed and lime juice are kept in a boiling claypot under a stool (with a central opening) and the woman sits over this to receive the steam. Antiseptic and and astringent, it firms and strengthens muscles too.

A perfectionist by nature, the Datin is a very open-hearted and generous person, more than happy to share her family's formulations with the world. Her motto is "the more you give, the more you receive" – and, as anyone who knows her will testify, she is true to her words in life.

Her first book on Malay midwifery was launched in 2007 and has been a huge success. With tips for pre- and post-natal women and a host of at-home remedies, the book is very informative. When reprimanded that she is giving away too many secrets, she replied: "The information in the book contains only about 10 percent of my knowledge; there is much more where these recipes came from!"

One of the Datin's specialist rituals is the Royal Malay Treatment which she formulated with her daughter-in-law (see previous pages). Taking elements of *ukup* therapy (steam or sauna therapy), it centres around the treatment of the human reproductive system believed by Malays to be the *penyawa* (life force) of the human body. Based on old recipes from her family treasure trove, it is a marvelous healing treat for any couple.

Left Part of the aroma pedi includes a masque of Moor mud, a jet black clay that is very high in minerals. Hydrating and purifying, not to mention detoxifying, it is followed by the application of a balm that comprises lavender, rosemary, menthol and pine oil and an invigorating calf and foot massage.

Feet are often neglected in general day-to-day care; an aroma pedicure at Spa Village brings life back to tired toes.

EAST MEETS WEST   Celebrating the cosmopolitan nature of Malaysia's capital city, Spa Village Kuala Lumpur also offers a number of Western treatments and some unusual mixes that combine Western know-how with tropical ingredients. The Trade Winds ritual is a case in point: it begins with an exfoliating papaya and calamansi scrub for ladies and a red clay scrub for men, but is followed by a Swedish massage session and a European facial. The skin softening qualities of papaya enzymes have been employed in Asia for at least two centuries; here it is mixed with a gentle citrus hint for added cleansing.

Other less tropical treatments include cellulite-busting spirulina and seaweed wraps, the use of caviar in some facials, hot stone, aromatherapy and *lomi-lomi* massage and an aromatic pedicure that utilises purifying, re-mineralising Moor mud and a harbal balm. In the city where everyone has to put their best foot forward, feet tend to be overlooked: they tire easily and swell, so this particular aroma pedi helps to stimulate circulation as well as revitalise aching feet.

Left A soothing and antiseptic eucaplyptus foot bath commences the treatment. Refreshing for tired feet, it prepares skin for the treatment to follow.

An à la carte Experience: Sensory Exploration

Given in a darkened, quiet room as an antidote to the noise, pollution and stress of downtown Kuala Lumpur, the unique 50-minute Sensory Exploration is an innovative addition to the Spa Village repertoire. Designed to put guests in touch with their senses and to awaken awareness through sounds, sights, smells, tastes and textures, the ritual also heightens guests' connection with their immediate environment, all the time helping a bonding with the inner self.

Offered as a private ritual or as a group activity, guests are encouraged to give themselves up to a specially trained therapist who guides the entire process. Simple meditation focusing on spirituality starts the procedure, then the therapist stimulates guests' senses through aromatherapy (sense of smell), ceiling lights changing colours (sense of sight), a floor vibrating with music (sense of touch and sound) and the eating of small morsels of salt, bitter gourd, lemon and dates (various senses of taste). People report that the sequence is simultaneously quietly peaceful, yet unusually exhilarating.

As the therapist gives guests the various items to feel, smell or taste, nerve endings send reflexes to the brain; the cerebral cortex then translates this information into specific sensory categories, thereby facilitating a heightened awareness. Being in touch with the five senses has been proven to have medical and mental benefits, and guests often report a sense of euphoria after the session.

The finale to this unusual offering is a scalp, neck, shoulder and foot massage that helps to slow down and relax the client. Guests are given a healing stone as a parting gift and they exit the room somehow lighter and without worries – ready to face the frenzied streets of Kuala Lumpur again.

Right above A specially trained guide takes a client on her journey of heightened awareness in a darkened, somewhat mysterious, environment.
Right Given lying down, the massage finale soothes and calms the accelerated nervous system.

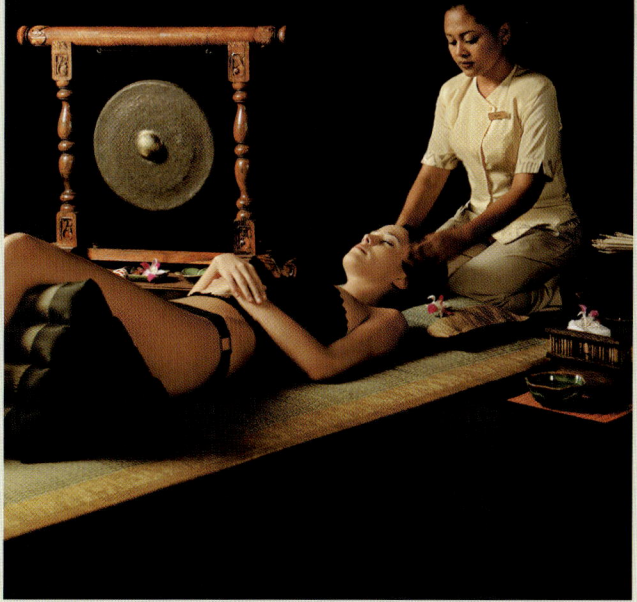

Small, yet perfectly formed, this urban spa has all the elements necessary for de-stressing: quiet, calm, luxury and stillness.

Right top Three outdoor cabanas set adjacent the pool are the outdoor equivalents of spa suites. **Right middle** Retail equates with relaxation, shopping with therapy, right? The spa shop has a wonderful range of Spa Village products along with resort wear and more.

Right bottom The spa reception area combines efficiency with welcoming smiles. Decor is in neutral tones with silk screen ornamentation and dark wood – so as to facilitate healing and relaxation. **Opposite** Spa rooms are luxurious with Chinese silks and comfortable beds.

AN URBAN OASIS   There is no doubt that urban lifestyles take their toll, with pollution and hectic schedules contributing to high levels of stress. It has now been proven that natural ingredients are effective counter-balances to modern-day ills such as tension, premature aging, tiredness and depression. This gives an added impetus for the busy urbanite to take advantage of the tranquility that can be had at Spa Village Kuala Lumpur.

   In addition to the beautiful pool and deck, many treatment rooms have private en-suite gardens (see opposite) with ample-sized plunge pools, so hydrotherapy is another option. As water is the source of existence, it always has a role in the spa. When it is used in Asia with natural ingredients and age-old purifcation practices, it is particularly effective.

A Sanctuary In The Hills

SPA VILLAGE CAMERON HIGHLANDS

Set high in the hills in an untouched jungle environment, Spa Village Cameron Highlands is blessed with a unique botanical heritage. Surrounded by many unusual species and plenty of better-known ones, it draws from its vicinity for more than inspiration. In the same way that the area's ancient inhabitants relied on their environment for sustenance, the spa succours guests with the bounty of the forest.

The focus at the spa is on the area's natural storehouse: Many jungle ingredients – used by the local Semai aboriginals for centuries in day-to-day remedies – find their way into exotic healing and pampering treatments. Similarly, tea, a plant grown extensively in plantations across the Cameron's rolling hillsides, is used for its anti-oxidant properties in the signature bath – and more. Such plants, along with other locally-grown fruits and flowers that thrive in the area's temperate elevations are combined with the healing hands of local therapists.

A haven of quiet away from the mayhem of Malaysia's cities, the Cameron Highlands offers an experience a little like stepping back in time. Diversions are few, which is perhaps why the resort in which the spa is located was at one time a sanatorium.

If today's spas have replaced the infirmaries of the past, there's no doubt that Spa Village Cameron Highlands can broker real wellness results. Recommending a daily diet of gentle treks and a variety of spa treatments, it is relaxing in the extreme.

Left With indoor and outdoor treatment areas and plenty of relaxation space, Spa Village Cameron Highlands, set in an emerald landscape, is calm and quiet.

Above Fresh young green tea shoots aren't just used for a refreshing beverage; they make for exciting spa ingredients too. Signature tea baths are a special here.

Right top In a bid to educate guests who are unable or don't have the time to experience the jungle first hand, the resort's naturalist Shahril is constructing a conservatory on three levels behind the hotel. Entirely planted with specimens he has collected in the immediate locality, it is a natural herbarium of plants ranging from orchids to ferns, palms, gingers and other lesser known species.

Opposite Shahril takes a client on a nature walk, pointing out both poisonous and healing plants; often they can be both simultaneously. **Above and right** Three species commonly used by local jungle inhabitants for healing. *Clockwise from top left*, the *dukung anak* plant, *petai* seeds used for kidney problems and *jering*, the fruit of which removes bladder stones.

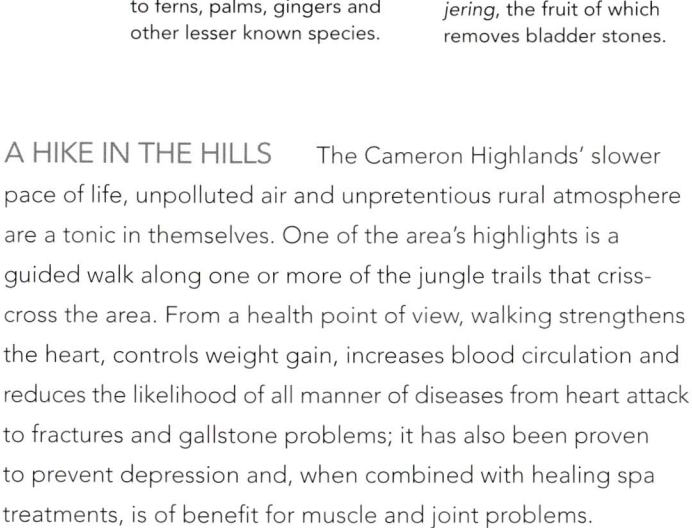

A HIKE IN THE HILLS   The Cameron Highlands' slower pace of life, unpolluted air and unpretentious rural atmosphere are a tonic in themselves. One of the area's highlights is a guided walk along one or more of the jungle trails that criss-cross the area. From a health point of view, walking strengthens the heart, controls weight gain, increases blood circulation and reduces the likelihood of all manner of diseases from heart attack to fractures and gallstone problems; it has also been proven to prevent depression and, when combined with healing spa treatments, is of benefit for muscle and joint problems.

The Cameron Highlands Resort's resident naturalist, Shahril Kamarulzaman, a plant biologist who has been studying the fauna of the lower montane forests in Malaysia for over 20 years, is also the resort's hiking guide. He considers the Cameron Highlands a "hotspot of biological diversity" amongst Malaysia's various habitats and says that it has been somewhat neglected over the years from a botanical perspective. Today, however, it is finally getting the recognition it deserves.

Along the trails around the hotel in the lower montane level (1,000 to 1,600 m; 3,280 to 5,250 feet), where specifically oak and laurel flourish, there is an extraordinary variety of plant life. Two new species have been discovered in the last year – one orchid and one herb – and Shahril believes that more are sure to follow. It is just a matter of time.

PORTRAIT OF A HEALER: A Hands-on Healer

Although she doesn't come from a family of herbalists or healers, 41-year-old Sairani Mohd Sa'ad has more than a touch of green in her fingers when it comes to adapting plant-based formulations into efficacious treatments. A trainer and consultant at Spa Village, Sairani is responsible for the inspiring traditional Malay therapies at the group's series of spas.

Sairani reckons she was about four years old when she first showed an interest in plants. "As a child my hobby was gardening and learning about plants," she remembers, "My favourite was ylang-ylang – it was not even famous then – and I used to pick it from my Quran teacher's garden every day."

Her fascination with Malay healing began when she was introduced to her husband's family and their living apothecary of herbal formulations and treatments (see page 67). As a young mother with small children, she frequently dipped into this treasure trove of botanical recipes handed down through the generations ("You could say I have a lot of experience in how to take care of oneself after delivery!" she laughs) – and once her children were older, she accepted a job offer from Spa Village to set up the Malay-based spa at Pangkor Laut. This was followed by her research and formulation of the Semai Treatments and Tungku Batu at Spa Village Cameron Highlands – and other Malay treatments at the various spas.

Relying on her mother-in-law's advice and blessings is important, but many of the imaginative spa sequences are Sairani's own work. "I work with my husband's cousin in product formulation," she explains, "Usually we take the base of an original family recipe, or in the case of the Semai treatments some of their herbal remedies, then add other ingredients and scents. We play around with textures and properties to create products that retain tradition."

However, it should also be noted that Sairani is often an innovator as well as a replicator. Many of Spa Village's products and sequences are the result of her creativity: new formulations that combine her knowledge of plant properties with her inherent intuition.

Acknowledging that she is more hands-on and her mother-in-law more of a mentor, Sairani admits that sometimes she doesn't quite know how she ends up with a finished recipe. "Listen is the only word I can come up with," she says, "I listen with all the senses that I have and, after that, I start to do the research, make combinations and take it from there."

Above Sairani Mohd Sa'ad, pictured in the environs of Spa Village Kuala Lumpur. Sairani is responsible for most of the Malay therapies in the various spa venues. **Right** Sairani has five children yet remains slim and fit; she puts this down to the traditional Malay post-natal therapies she used after each birth. She used the *boros puteri* scrub, the ingredients of which are shown here, to cleanse, firm and whiten the skin on the abdomen after each pregnancy.

The surrounding jungle and tea plantations form the basis for
many of the therapies at Spa Village Cameron Highlands.

A BOTANICAL HAVEN   Naturally, the area's indigenous inhabitants, Malaysia's so-called *orang asli* or "original people" have known about and employed these vast natural reserves for centuries. When William Cameron, a British colonial government surveyor, "discovered" the series of green plateaus on a mapping expedition in 1885, he (and later British developers) largely ignored the local forest dwellers. The subsequent commercialisation of the land for tea plantations (see pages 86–89), market gardening and flower nurseries meant they had to retreat deeper into the jungle – where they continued the natural rhythm of their lives in tune with and attuned to nature.

Fortuitously, Spa Village personnel managed to form a relationship with a family of Semai, one of the forest-dwelling aboriginals, whose knowledge of the area's *materia medica* is unparalleled (see overleaf). To the Semai, each and every forest herb and plant has a specific use, be it medicinal, edible or poisonous. It may look like a weed to the outsider, but to the Semai it is a precious resource.

Over millennia, Semai elders have passed down their valuable botanical secrets from generation to generation, keeping intact an ancient culture of healing. Luckily, Spa Village is now able to share some of them with the wider world.

Left Water, naturally, is considered the elixir of the jungle – and indeed of the spa. All Semai treatments at Spa Village Cameron Highlands use this enlivening element – in abundance.
Above A selection of raw ingredients that are used in the Jungle Secrets of Anti-Aging for Her ritual: these include the green *Piper betle* leaf, a good cleanser, as well as a number of rhizomes, roots and seeds. Jasmine blooms provide the sweet scent.

SOPHISTICATED SEMAI TREATMENTS   In keeping with the group's intention of building lasting relationships with local people, Spa Village has been lucky to have this family of Semai as mentors in the setting up of the spa at Cameron Highlands Resort. Many treatments use elements of Semai knowledge along with modern, tried-and-tested remedies and techniques. From a guest's point of view, it feels just right to treat yourself to a scrub, wrap, facial, bath or massage when you know the fresh ingredients have come directly from the surrounding jungle.

Two rituals, the Tok Batin Mystical Tradition for Him and the Jungle Secrets of Anti-Aging for Her, are based on ancient Semai health remedies. Both take full advantage of aromatic root and bark extracts, leaves, seeds and juices used by the Semai in their traditional therapies – and both make for powerful and rejuvenating healing. By reviving and preserving these age-old recipes and combining them with modern-day research, Spa Village is ensuring their very survival.

Both rituals use a variety of forest treasures that include rambutan bark, sappanwood, henna, tea and betel leaves, ginger, cumin seeds, cinnamon and Kaffir lime. They are designed to cleanse, moisturise, promote healthy circulation of the blood as well as remove negative energy. The ladies' sequence includes both a sitz bath as a monthly anti-aging maintenance for ladies and an anti-aging bath to firm muscles soothe irritation, moisturise skin and reduce any swelling.

A FAMILY OF SEMAI: HELPERS AND HERBALISTS

The Semai, one of the 18 ethnic subgroups of *orang asli* or "original people" of Peninsular Malaysia, tend to live in and near the Cameron Highlands. Indigenous to the area, most continue to live in the forest as subsistence farmers relying on the land for their food, medicine and fuel. As with other aboriginal peoples, they see the land as a living entity: it is a sacred space, full of spirits.

As with many traditional societies, Semai elders are given respect and precedence; in return, they share their knowledge with their children and grandchildren as and when necessary. Their advice may be sought at any time and on any subject. In matters of illness and health, for example, the elders reign supreme. With extensive knowledge of the plant life around them, they are both herbalists and teachers, passing on prescriptions and remedies that they, themselves, received from their elders. Their apothecary contains tonics, poultices, lotions and juices that may be taken both internally and externally. Barks, roots, leaves and more are all utilised.

Believing that the forest is communal, they do not charge for their services, but freely share prescriptions for stomach and head aches, wounds, bites, broken bones and allergies. They have also formulated a number of remedies for pregnant and post-natal women to stop excess bleeding and promote the shrinking of the uterus after delivery. For men, there are virility boosts and body strengtheners.

Spa Village personnel made contact with a member of an extended Semai family, Rahman aka Bahtuin, an assistant *tok batin* (chief) of a village deep within the forest. Both his mother and mother-in law are midwives and many of the elders are proficient in herbal healing. After discussions, this family decided to share some of their wellness recipes, and these have subsequently been adapted into treatments at Spa Village Cameron Highlands.

In recent years, developed countries have expressed a renewed interest in plant-based medicines; a distrust of synthetic chemicals with their side effects has led many people to desire more "natural" solutions to health problems. Unfortunately, most of the Semai's folk remedies are undocumented, and there is a real danger that much of their knowledge is fast disappearing. Preserving them for posterity is vital – and by working with Rahman's family and reinterpreting their age-old formulations into new spa treatments, Spa Village is helping with this vital task.

Top A member of a Semai tribe uses a traditional blow pipe for hunting.
Above A Semai village built on a ridge not far from Spa Village Cameron Highlands.
Right A selection of herbs, barks, flowers and fruits used in some of the Semai rituals at the spa; they are displayed on a mat woven by Semai women.

The fairy-tale, mossy montane forest of the Cameron Highlands provides medicines, food, sustenance and succour to its inhabitants.

Left Honey is collected and traded by the Semai: the dark variety is taken from the inner part of the *tualang* tree where bees have constructed a natural hive; the lighter one comes from a hanging nest of young bees. Often used in spa treatments, honey is an effective humectant.

In addition, the powerful combination of herbs acts as a general tonic, leaving the guest feeling younger and fitter, ready to face the world! Similarly, you can imagine the scent from the Semai scrub when you know what goes into it: nutmeg, clove, galangal, turmeric, a host of lesser known barks, roots and rhizomes, rice powder, jasmine and green tea, a potent combination if ever there was one. When smoothed over the body, the mix penetrates deep into the subcutaneous layers to promote the growth of new cells, cleanse and firm skin and whiten skin tone.

There is something special about being scrubbed, bathed and massaged to a state of eco-bliss knowing all the while that your body and mind are de-toxing 100 percent naturally. In addition, you feel secure knowing that the powerful combination of natural organics is one that has been used successfully and safely for eons.

Above and opposite top Much more than a rumble in the jungle, the Semai rituals for him and her are totally authentic recreations of traditional forest dwellers' therapeutic practices. *Clockwise from top:* Used in both a sitz bath and an anti-aging bath, this combination of herbs and salts firms muscles, reduces irritation, and moisturises skin. The scrub is deeply penetrating and is offered, with slight adaptations, for both men and women.

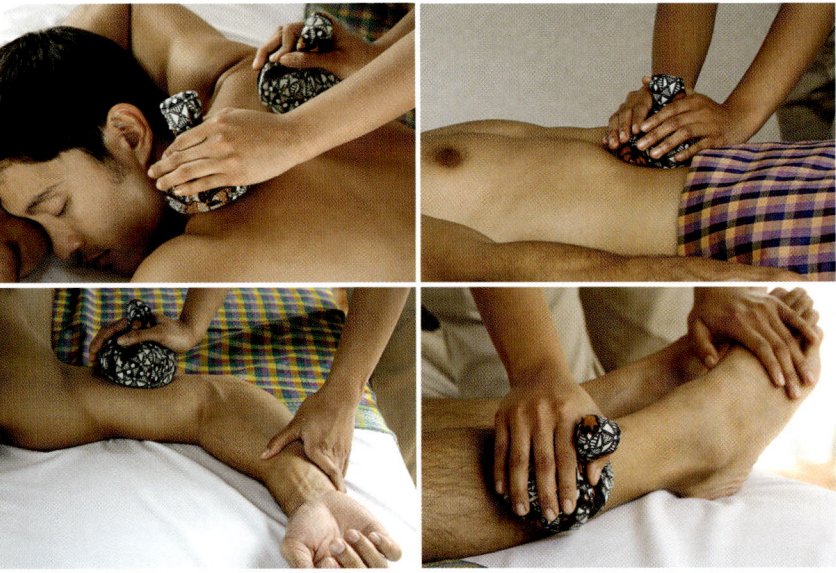

Left Key points to apply hot stones in the Tunku Batu massage are neck, abdomen, calves and arms to heat muscles and tissues. **Right** The stones are made from seven layers of red clay, moulded and baked for intensity, and are wrapped in a *mengkudu* or Indian mulberry leaf, then further wrapped in cloth. The leaf is a natural detoxifier and, when combined with the heat from the stones, helps speed up blood circulation.

BOTANIC BLISS: A SPA MENU TO REMEMBER

Another therapy that has its roots in ancient *orang asli* and Malay culture is a particular form of heated stone therapy. Formulated from the tradition of massaging hot stones on to a woman's abdomen after birth to help the womb and muscles shrink back to their original size, it has been adapted at Spa Village Cameron Highlands to increase strength and vitality. Called Tunku Batu Massage (*batu* translates as "stone"; a *tungku* is the hearth where the stone is traditionally heated up), it's an ancient but effective formulation from the Malay heirloom.

First of all the client is vigorously massaged with a warm, spicy medicated ointment known as *minyak lumur sakti*, consisting of coconut oil, cloves, nutmeg, galangal and lemon-grass, then the heated stones are pressed into key locations on the body to loosen tense muscles, alleviate pain, reduce inflammation, break down excess fats and cellulite and to promote a deep feeling of utter relaxation. Its benefits are deep-seated; its application warm and nurturing.

In addition to the *orang asli* inspired rituals, Spa Village Cameron Highlands offers a number of other treatments based around plants that thrive in this cool elevated area. Each is designed to bring the body and mind back to equilibrium, be it through detoxification, rejuvenation, hydration, nourishment, or a combination of the above. What could be more beguiling than gracious Malaysian care, loving hands and sophisticated treatments utilising honey, strawberries, tea, roses, and more?

"We have a lot to learn from our natural heritage," says Shahril, resident naturalist at Spa Village Cameron Highlands. "The forest holds many secrets."

The Queen of Flowers

Transplanting a little bit of Scotland into Malaysia's hillsides wasn't too difficult a task for James Duncan Robertson when he designed the Cameron Highlands' first rose garden in 1934. The cool climate and fertile soil made it ideal for rose cultivation, and today there are more than 600 varieties growing on its terraced slopes. The fragrant, buff apricot Diamond Jubilee rose is 65 years old and the deep velvety red Crimson Glory has a scent like port wine. Robertson's widow still lives on the property and makes rose petal jam and rose syrup, amongst other home-made goodies.

Naturally, rose petals also make wonderful spa products: They've been used for thousands of years for their essential oil, their scent, their skin softening properties – and their sheer beauty. Paying tribute to these Cameron-grown roses, Spa Village Cameron Highlands offers a number of treatments using the blooms of the yellow champagne rose: try bathing in the heartening aroma of rose, or opt for an aromatic massage or gentle body exfoliation. You'll emerge refreshed and rose-scented for sure.

Above, clockwise from left Being a temperate climate herb, mint grows in profusion in the highlands, so it is easily harvested for this enlivening scrub. The mix, using mint, thyme and some deeply exfoliating ingredients, is also offered as a wrap if the client prefers. Strawberries always bring to mind long English summers, so are an ideal accompaniment to spa treatments in what was once an old English hill station. Both yoghurt and strawberries are high in natural alpha-hydroxy acids, so this sweet-smelling polish leaves skin texture soft and shining.

Mint, a temperate herb that grows in profusion around the hotel, is another local plant that forms the basis for a scrub, wrap, bath and muscle-relief body massage. Known for its tangy taste and scent, mint improves blood circulation and gives run-down immune systems a well-deserved boost. Fresh strawberries also find their way from the dessert menu to the spa menu: high in vitamin C, both leaves and fruit are often used in poultices on wounds as they are a useful blood coagulant. In the spa, they're combined with yoghurt and crushed oatmeal for a refreshing body buff to leave skin softened and refined. Or try the fresh-from-the-fields scented massage: here, aroma and touch combine to rehydrate, relax and rejuvenate.

Flowers are an obvious addition to any spa, and at Spa Village Cameron Highlands, they include chrysanthemums with their long history of medicinal uses, and roses, known the world over for their scent (see left). Both flourish in the cooler climes of the highlands, so are literally plucked and used immediately in baths, massages and beauty treatments. Similarly fresh are the newly-picked young tea shoots and leaves used in the signature tea bath offered before every treatment: also, added to some other therapies, tea plays a central role at Spa Village Cameron Highlands.

Left Two open-sided cabanas (one pictured here) and six treatment rooms, some with private baths, comprise the facilities at the luxurious spa.

Far left Afternoon tea and strawberries at the hotel.
Left The Cameron Highlands Resort, built in mock Tudor style in black and white, resembles an English country estate. Naturally it fronts a 9-hole golf course.
Right Velvety rolling hill-sides planted with emerald tea bushes resemble patch-work quilts from a distance: their tea leaves have found new life in spa treatments.

TEA: A RITUAL AND A HEALER

There is nothing more quintessentially British than afternoon tea, sandwiches and scones served with strawberry jam and cream round a roaring fire. Usually the wind is howling and the rain lashing outside, as families all over the UK partake of an afternoon cuppa. In keeping with the colonials' predilection for creating little pockets of home in their postings overseas, the Cameron Highlands was developed as a 19th-century hill station, a refuge where perspiration-soaked civil servants could retire to relax and savour cooler temperatures.

Such hill stations spanned the empire, from the hills of India and Sri Lanka to Burma and Malaysia. With mock-Tudor cottages, English-style gardens planted with roses and other perennials, golf courses and a local club, they resembled mini recreations of Surrey or Sussex villages transplanted to the tropics. Offering both climactic and emotional stability, they represented a little piece of "home".

Because of their elevation, these hill stations also became home to massive plantations of tea with hectares of stocky *Camellia sinensis* bushes replacing the indigenous forests. Such plantations are ubiquitous in the vicinity of the Cameron Highlands Resort: A visit to one is an educational experience (see overleaf), while a walk amongst the undulating hillsides makes a refreshing change from a jungle trek.

Tea is now grown commercially all over Malaysia for the ever expanding green, black, white and oolong tea market – but at Spa Village Cameron Highlands it's much more than a traditional afternoon event.

The Cameron Highlands' fertile slopes, cool climate and plentiful rainfall are perfect for growing tea. Transplanted to the spa, tea is anti-oxidant, nourishing, cleansing and skin-softening.

Realizing that tea has real anti-aging benefits, Spa Village's yellow rose tea bath combines the rejuvenating properties of tea with the beautiful scent of the champagne rose.

Rich in antioxidant polyphenols, tea promotes skin elasticity and cell growth when applied externally. It is anti-bacterial, astringent and anti-inflammatory and the extract is often added to skincare products to reduce fine lines, wrinkles, puffiness and large pores. In a bath, tea leaves help to neutralise free radicals, increase cell longevity, strengthen the immune system and help protect the skin against aging.

Spa therapists have embraced these benefits in a number of treatments: in addition to the signature tea bath, there's a yellow rose tea both for scent-sual relaxation, an uplifting mint tea bath to stimulate, cool and help with muscle aches, and a strawberry tea bath to ease nervous tension and stress.

Bathing has always been integral to Asian culture, both for spiritual purification and cleansing, so integrating a bath before every treatment at Spa Village Cameron Highlands is a natural step. It gives guests a boost of positive energy and fills the air with an enlivening herbaceous aroma. In addition, water is always nurturing, tranquilising and soul-soothing.

Above In Asia, bathing is seen as a purification rite on more than the merely physical level; at Spa Village Cameron Highlands, tea is a key ingredient in the signature bath given before each treatment.

Below Tea is linked to cell rejuvenation as it is rich in antioxidants; placing tea bags over the eyes helps reduce puffiness, bags and dark circles, and can also be very relaxing while another therapy takes place.

The Tea Connection

Members of staff at the Cameron Highlands Resort are more than happy to organise a visit to the BOH tea plantation at nearby Sungei Palas. It's a worthwhile trip not only for tea aficionados, but to drink in views of the velvety plantation slopes. The resort is surrounded by such plantations, and the healing, restorative properties of tea are a key ingredient in the Spa Village repertoire.

Sungei Palas is a high altitude, frost-free environment that has well-drained soil and abundant rainfall – perfect for growing *Camellia sinensis*. The ancient Chinese are known to have been the first people to drink tea for its medicinal value and by the 17th century it had become popular in the West. The habit spread over Asia in colonial times as the British, French and Dutch established plantations from the Sri Lankan and Indian highlands to areas in Malaysia, Indonesia and Indo-China.

The BOH tea company was the first to be established in the Cameron Highlands in 1929 by John Archibald Russell; today it is run by a third-generation member of the founding family and produces some four million kilograms of tea every year. With four sites in Malaysia – two in the Cameron Highlands and two more at lower altitudes – it has an impressive 1,200 hectares (2,965 acres) of planted tea in total. A family-run business, the tea is mainly grown for export, although it is popular in Malaysia too.

There is something both primitive and romantic about a tea factory, and a guided tour of the five-pronged tea production process is a fascinating experience. First the young green shoots (and darker, older leaves) are picked from the shrubs, then transported to the factory for processing. This includes withering (reducing the moisture), rolling (crushing the leaf cells), fermenting (oxidation, when the leaves turn from green to copper), drying via heat and sorting. In the latter process, stalks and fibres are extracted from the bulk to be used as secondary fertilisation, while the rest is set aside for packaging.

Crushed tea dust is used for tea bags, larger cuttings are used for loose-leaf tea – and, of course, the cream of the crop is reserved for Spa Village treatments!

Above A tea picker at work with heavenly views over the slopes of the BOH tea plantation behind. Tea tasting is taken as seriously as wine tasting, with stringent controls and timing for each brew; here BOH employee Parthipidri explains the ropes to an interested novice.
Below From field to factory, the various processes of tea production have changed little over the decades; it is still labour-intensive.

AN AIR OF TRANQUILITY   In fact, the environs of the spa (and the hotel as a whole) also help to give guests a truly tranquil experience. The simple spa suites, many with attendant claw-foot tubs, and two outdoor cabanas are designed to help guests redress mind/body imbalances – and really relax. In addition, there's also a fully equipped gymnasium and plenty of lounging space. Fronted by an elegant bubbling water feature with the jungle as a backdrop, the spa and its facilities ease guests into a more comfortable state of being.

Post-treatment tea time in the hotel completes the spa experience more than adequately. Here, the flavour is distinctly nostalgic, with French doors, plantation shutters, wood-beamed ceilings and colonial furniture creating an ambience in keeping with the architecture of the hotel. It's not surprising that the Cameron Highlands has been described as "a little piece of England in Asia" – and the resort more than happily perpetuates the atmosphere of those long-gone days.

Left The spa premises itself is a beguiling cocktail of colonial chic and modern-day amenities. The cool palette of champagne, gold and white is welcoming and easy on the eye.
Right After a spa session, invigorating hike or round of golf, the hotel lounge is the scene for stylish escapism.

The atmosphere, service and attention to detail at Cameron Highlands Resort evoke an era when elegance, luxury and bespoke facilities were a given.

Unmistakably Malay

SPA VILLAGE TANJONG JARA

Set on the Terengganu coast on the eastern seaboard of the Malaysian Peninsula, Spa Village Tanjong Jara is a sanctuary of the senses in more ways than one. Offering a number of unique restorative treatments handed down by ancient Malay healers using a plethora of local ingredients, it is a harmonious balance of luxury and eco purity. In addition, there are the added attractions of hiking in the rainforest, snorkeling off a nearby island in the South China Sea, a session of meditative exercise on the beach, and simply chilling in salubrious surrounds.

Of all the group's properties, Tanjong Jara is indelibly anchored in its milieu. Partly because it is quite isolated, and partly because it seeks to offer guests a totally authentic experience,

90 percent of the staff comes from nearby villages. Their aim is to impart the Malay philosophy of *sucimurni* to the guest: a way of life that embraces purity of spirit, wellness and revitalisation.

Over the centuries, families of healers from local villages have amassed a rich body of knowledge regarding wellbeing; using the rich bounty from the surrounding forests, they have formulated some extraordinarily powerful healing remedies. Spa Village Tanjong Jara personnel have been fortunate to adapt and revive some of these traditions.

The result is an environment dedicated to quiet relaxation, restoration and rejuvenation. Delve into it with an open heart, and you'll be sure to emerge nurtured and revived.

Left The arc of crystalised sand that makes up the bay at Tanjong Jara is lined with casuarina trees on one side and the South China Sea on the other.

Above The tropical roselle bloom is the signature ingredient of the spa. Here, it is beautifully displayed on a Malay brass tray with the scrub that takes its name.

The concept of *sucimurni*, which embraces tranquility and purity through wholesome living, permeates throughout the whole resort.

AUTHENTIC ARCHITECTURE IN AN ENERGISING ENVIRONMENT

Every spa needs an environment that is at once restful and rejuvenating. Tanjong Jara is no exception. As the first deluxe tourist accommodation built on Malaysia's eastern coast, its primary aims were to sustain and preserve the local architectural heritage, encourage local crafts and establish a mutually supportive relationship with local communities. This it has succeeded in – and the addition of its ground-breaking spa which borrows freely from local traditions and personnel has only furthered this integrative mission.

The crescent-shaped beach around which the hotel and spa nestle is an inspiring environment for healing. Home to nesting grounds for leatherback and green turtles, it also serves as an ideal exercise and *silat* practice arena. Just back from the beach are the resort's accommodations: Modelled after *istanas*, wooden palaces of great beauty and dignity built by the earlier Sultans of east coast Malaysia, they are comfortable, yet elegant. Comprising mainly two-storey hardwood buildings, elevated on stilts, they mimic the pavilion style of the region with open-sided rooms, intricate latticework and steeply pitched roofs.

All are set in abundant tropical gardens where an ethos of peace and harmony prevails. There is a blissful absence of commercialism; instead, there are spa treatments and healing programmes, reflecting pools, scarlet sunbirds amongst the ornamental plants, and, in the gardens at night, the exotic timbre of an evocative *gamelan* player.

Opposite The stunning arc of crystalline sand that comprises the bay at Tanjong Jara is integral to the spa experience at the resort.
This page The complex of wooden buildings in landscaped gardens won the Aga Khan Award for Architecture in 1983 for replicating the motif of 17th-century Sultans' palaces. The prize, given by the Aga Khan Trust for Culture in Geneva, honours buildings in Muslim communities that demonstrate architectural excellence. Utilising local artifacts, materials and craftsmen, the resort incorporates aspects of Malay traditions to provide the ultimate in luxurious living. Rooms are a mixture of *belian* wood, timber and teak, while two restaurants and a poolside bar give an authentic taste of the region's culture and spirit.

Caressed with sea breezes, the spa is cool,
tranquil and tropical – an oasis of calm.

Left and opposite Voted Best Hotel Spa in Asia-Pacific and the Indian Subcontinent by the UK's *Condé Nast Traveller* and ranked number two in their list of World's Top 26 Spas, Spa Village Tanjong Jara combines healing treatments of integrity with an environment that is truly Malay. Elegantly crafted spa suites, copious water bodies and local materials combine to create a natural habitat for healing. This traditional-styled gateway or *pintu gerbang* marks the entrance to the spa facility. A tranquil long water feature is situated about two feet away from it.

A SANCTUARY FOR THE SENSES – MALAY STYLE

If the resort's strapline is "unmistakably Malay", the watchword at the spa is "wellbeing". The recipient of numerous awards, including the prize for Most Innovative Spa from the UK's prestigious *Tatler* magazine in 2007, Spa Village Tanjong Jara is integral to the overall experience at the resort.

Situated in a sprawling complex of structures, paths and gardens with a beautiful elongated reflecting pool at the entrance, the gym and therapy centre lead off from the beach. Pandanus-and-palm fringed walkways connect the various buildings, while pan-Asian urns and flower-filled basins provide

decorative detail. Indoor-outdoor treatment pavilions are a heady mix of local stone, marble and wood with vine-clad pergolas shading from the sun and scented outdoor sunken baths providing cool. Overhead, mischievous macaque monkeys swing in the tree canopy like miniature acrobatic urchins.

First of all, guests are welcomed at a dedicated reception where they sign in, then they are led to an open-sided *warong* for pre-treatment tea. Here, they are able to discuss their preferences, likes and dislikes with members of staff, many of whom come from local families who frequently practice massage at home. They are also able to view the cornucopia

Spa Village Tanjong Jara

Left A pavilion-style spa suite features typical Malay detailing such as wooden fretwork, a soaring roof and elegant sarong-clad massage beds. Extremely spacious, they are open sided, yet very private. **Below** A cup of post-treatment tea is given in the *warong* where guests are able to further relax after their therapy.

of herbs, oils and locally-produced products that are employed at the spa – and discuss any health issues. A medical questionnaire is compulsory, so therapists have a comprehensive picture of the overall health of their clients.

From here, it is a short walk to one of seven therapy suites, all of which are set in fragrant gardens. Each has two massage beds, plenty of space, beautiful tropical plantings – and is especially suited to couples. Unsurprisingly, many of Tanjong Jara's guests are honeymooners; fortuitously, there are plenty of romantic treatments to be taken *à deux*.

Massage at Spa Village Tanjong Jara honours the village massage approach, but sometimes combines it with hot sand or energizing flowers or herbs.

 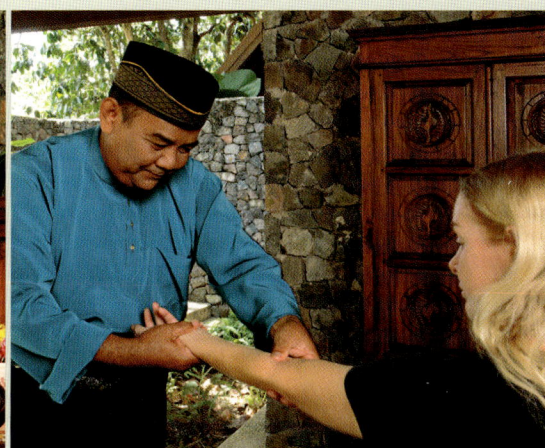

Portrait of a Healer: A Mountain of a Man

Spa Village Tanjong Jara's resident head masseuse, 54-year old Pak Yahya, is no newcomer to healing. Residing in a nearby *kampong* (village), he comes from a family of healers, having learned his massage skills directly from his grandmother.

A jovial person by nature, Pak Yahya has a big build but a soft heart. His forefathers were all masseurs, and his skills are partly innate, partly learnt. With many years of experience under his belt, his expertise is legendary in the surrounding region. He is renowned for being able to detect knots and tightness in muscles and having the ability to release them.

Pak Yahya's signature massage has been described as "bone-loosening", "simply divine" and one client describes the experience thus: "I feel that he is scanning the body when he works on me – and he invariably finds those knots that need attention".

With wide hands and plenty of physical strength, Pak Yahya uses a "big palm technique" that is guaranteed to leave you feeling like you're floating on air. Consisting of long, kneading strokes using thumb and palm pressure, he sometimes employs elbows, feet and arms as well if necessary. His is a deep tissue massage that focuses on and facilitates the flow of blood in the *urat* or veins and arteries. He normally starts with the feet and ends with a head and scalp massage.

This is Malay Traditional Massage at its best: what differentiates the men from the boys, or Pak Yahya from his peers, is his 40 years of experience. Put simply, it sets him apart. Experience, as many a therapist knows and strives for, is often the best teacher.

Above left Pak Yahya's contribution to Malay massage was recognized in 2006 when he was awarded the winner of Best Therapist Awards at the annual Malaysian Spa & Wellness Awards.

Above right A therapeutic style that aims to remove energy blockages or tension within is the hallmark of Pak Yahya's technique. Both subtle and dynamic kneading pressure is used to stimulate muscles.

Asia's forests reveal their secrets in a host of therapeutic steams, scrubs, massages, tonics – and more.

Left Aromatherapy-based facial or body steams are a useful pick-me-up to try at home. At Spa Village Tanjong Jara the Malay steam is often given in a special zip-up bag that enables herbal oils to penetrate the skin faster than in the open air.

ANCIENT HEALING, MODERN TECHNIQUES

As befits its location, Spa Village Tanjong Jara focuses mainly on restorative Malay treatments that have been used in the country-side for centuries. Many are adaptations of local traditions, where the properties of indigenous botanicals have been harnessed for any number of different ailments.

Members of staff are always keen to explain the benefits of local plants to guests. In addition to such staples as Kaffir lime leaf, galangal and fenugreek, they'll also show you a bark that produces quinine (to counteract malaria) and a tree that has a white resin used to relieve symptoms of influenza and pneumonia. As is so often the case, what heals also hurts:

when heated, the latter turns into a black poison that is used on the tips of hunting darts by forest dwellers.

Arguably, the roselle flower, a dark red type of hibiscus that grows abundantly in the region, is the star of this spa. Widely known for its unique healing abilities, the plant was introduced to Malaysia from India and now grows wild throughout the peninsula: known locally as *asam paya*, *asam kumbang* or *asam susur* (*asam* translates as "sour"), it is high in vitamins and minerals and is used in local remedies for kidney disorders as it is a diuretic. Roselle is also known to lower blood-sugar levels, has anti-inflammatory properties and not only detoxifies and cleanses the body but also serves as an organic formulation

for anti-aging. It forms natural collagen and assists in vitamin absorption, thus improving the vitality of the skin, helping it to maintain a youthful glow.

Spa Village Tanjong Jara's signature Asam Roselle Experience lasts 100 minutes and begins with a relaxing massage using a blend of roselle, ginger, nutmeg, galangal and karoteno oil; full of vitamins A, C and E, it rejuvenates the body while simultaneously nourishing the skin. The long kneading strokes focus on the muscles and joints, gently easing away aches and pains. Followed by an aromatic, creamy scrub of roselle, rice and coconut oil to exfoliate, soften and refine skin, the treatment ends with a cup of refreshing roselle tea.

Above, clockwise from top left Originally native to India, *Hibiscus sabdariffa* L or the red roselle adapted quickly to Malaysia's fertile soil and tropical climate, and now grows in profusion all over the country. The ingredients for the scrub include rice and roselle flower; the massage has a hint of spicy nutmeg to boost circulation and help soothe muscle aches and rheumatic pain. The vivid rosy hue of the spa's signature roselle tea reveals a high concentration of antioxidants; it forms an anti-aging conclusion to the whole roselle experience. The scrub is a beautiful shade of strawberry pink: metabolically stimulating, it also oxygenates skin cells and flushes out toxins.

Left Some typical Malay ingredients used in one of the scented baths used in the couple's tretment: Local roots, herbs, flowers and fruits form the basis for profound cleansing, revitalising and purifying.

A TREAT FOR COUPLES   A very special half-day experience based on rituals traditionally given to brides and grooms before their marriage ceremony is a highlight at Spa Village Tanjong Jara. In Malaysia, the union of a man and his wife is considered a sacred event – and couples are cleansed, purified and prepared both physically and mentally in a number of ways before their wedding day.

The actual ceremony is renowned for its pomp and pageantry, and, on the day of the wedding, the couple are given the title of *Raja Sehari* which translates as King and Queen of the Day. To give Tanjong Jara couples a truly royal experience based on these age-old practices, a sequence of special body treatments has been formulated at the spa.

Beginning with a deep-tissue Malay massage that stimulates energy points and loosens and warms up muscles, the treatment also includes a conditioning hair treatment, a facial and body scrub, a scented milk bath and a traditional body steaming – all ending with an anti-aging tonic. Ingredients are fresh from nature – coconut, paddy stalks and pandanus for healthy hair; turmeric and galangal for scrubs; jasmine, rose and tropical magnolia for scented bathing; and Kaffir lime and fenugreek from an ancient recipe for a restorative bath. The latter is used locally to rebuild body strength and muscle firmness after injury; many of the therapists have prepared such a bath since childhood, so guests can relax in the invigorating blend secure in the knowledge that they are receiving a formula that is derived from centuries of tradition.

As with many Spa Village treatments, this carefully planned and executed experience is therapeutic, beautifying and relaxing. Whoever said that pampering can't be good for you?

Mandi Bunga: A Royal Ritual

In keeping with Spa Village tradition, Spa Village Tanjong Jara offers every guest a special pre-treatment ritual that honours local culture and heritage. Called the *mandi bunga*, a ceremony that originated in royal palaces where it was part of the formal procedures in the coronation of a new king, it is practiced by Malay healers to rid the body of negative energies. The ritual also forms part of coming-of-age celebrations and is administered to a Malay couple seven days before their wedding day.

At Tanjong Jara, a special procession with seven men carrying water jars or *buyong* takes place daily at 11 am from the lobby to the spa. Accompanied by seven women carrying brass trays with seven sweet-scented flowers, the *buyong* symbolise the seven sources of fresh water: namely rain, well water, river, stream, spring, waterfall and lake.

When the procession arrives at the spa, the water, along with the seven different flowers, is transferred into 175-year-old jars recovered from the Desaru shipwreck. They are then used in the *mandi bunga*, a special cleansing procedure where therapists bathe guests from head to toe seven times with the blessings of purity, sincerity, health, beauty, happiness, prosperity and longevity.

Many guests comment that celebrating Malaysia's age-old customs in this manner brings them closer to the heart of the country. And most are delighted with the memento they are presented with afterwards – a beautiful batik sarong.

Bathing, with its plethora of cleansing, invigorating and relaxing benefits, is the enlivening heart of the spa.

Left above Spa Village Tanjong Jara's *mandian raut pesona* is a traditional beautifying milk bath characterised by the heady aromas of clove and cardamom. Ingredients include almonds and honey to nourish and soften skin and more aromatic spices to warm skin, relieve mental fatigue, boost circulation and rejuvenate the entire body.

Left below The *boros puteri* scrub is an aromatic herbal body scrub using fresh ingredients such as turmeric and galangal to cleanse, firm and whiten the body. As it sloughs off dead skin cells, it promotes the growth of new cells beneath the surface.
Opposite Handcrafted bathrooms are a cool combo of wood and stone.

A LA CARTE EXPERIENCES: THERAPIES WITH A LOCAL FLAVOUR

In addition to the signature and couples' experiences, Spa Village Tanjong Jara offers a few à la carte treatments that take their inspiration from the local surroundings. Bathing is integral to Malay healing with spicy, aromatic baths prescribed for muscle soreness and aching limbs, lime baths used to energise and deodorise, and milk and flower baths an age-old beautifying option. Many of today's baths take their historical cue from royal bathing and steaming practices, where purification of the body was equated with mental, emotional and spiritual cleansing.

The bath menu at Spa Village Tanjong Jara comprises seven options, each designed for a different purpose. Always using freshly-blended ingredients, they leave bathers scented, refreshed or invigorated depending on the ingredients used. A particular favourite is the *mandian pulang semangat* for spiritual renewal: With lime as the main ingredient, it is an uplifting and invigorating bath. In Malay tradition, bathing in lime represents a symbolic relief of unwanted negative energies as lime is seen as the tangible link to the forces of the spiritual world. As such, the bath is characterised by a zesty aroma and has astringent properties as well as a high content of vitamin C. Cooling, cleansing and refreshing, it is extremely popular.

Other options include antioxidant baths for age repair, exotic ylang-ylang scented milk baths for lovers, and medicinal baths for muscle repair and the relief of jet-lag, amongst others. Taken in the gorgeous sunken baths in the private enclaves of the spa's pavilions, they're full of real wellness benefits.

The ocean is full of potent ingredients – minerals, trace elements, biological elements, amongst others – so a dip in its energising waters is both refreshing and healthful.

Left The therapeutic union of sea, sand, sea breezes and natural ingredients is uplifting for all the senses. Here, a therapist uses coconut milk and henna for healthy scalps and minds; the mix of ingredients is adapted from home hair care recipes.

Healthy hair is an integral part of Malay beauty and local women are renowned for their dark, thick and lustrous locks. Family remedies often include treatments, shampoos, rinses, lotions, infusions and pastes for beautifying, strengthening and improving the health of hair.

Spa Village Tanjong Jara offers two relaxing hair treatments: the *ulik nyiur*, that combines a yoghurt and coconut cream conditioner with a head massage, and the *ikal-ikal* that employs a specific scalp paste using henna and betel leaves. The former is helpful for dry scalp, dry hair, split ends and lacklustre hair as it adds shine and strength to hair, while the latter is beneficial for those who have dandruff, loss of hair, migraine or headaches. The paste is believed to draw out heat from the head and is accompanied by a hand massage.

Many guests who opt for a hair treatment often accompany it with a traditional Malay facial. Called the *muka berseri-seri*, it combines local massage techniques with a cleanse, tone, scrub, and mask, along with warmth from tiny pouches of steaming herbs that slowly relax facial muscles and inner tension. The various stages all use freshly pounded and blended ingredients (see right). As an added bonus the mask section is accompanied by a soothing hand massage.

Above It isn't surprising that many local women have such luminous complexions when you consider the ingredients that go into the traditional Malay facial: Ground rice, turmeric and galangal in the scrub; honey, yoghurt and medicated oil in the massage; white clay, egg yolk, rice and Malay herbs in the mask; and pandanus leaves and lemongrass in the steaming pouches. The finale is an application of aloe vera gel to cool and leave skin silky-smooth.

Far left The *jari-jemari* hand and foot soak uses fenugreek, blackseed, sea salt, henna and betel leaves as well as *uncang rendaman* in the soak, then employs a scrub of rice, turmeric and galangal. It ends with an invigorating Malay massage, culminating in the head and shoulder area.
Left top and below Returning the body, mind and spirit to equilibrium is the main function of any spa. Using local resources, such as the sand from the beach in heated pouches, does just that; it is also environmentally sustainable as the only other additions to the treatment are locally harvested herbs.

If you've endured the rigours of a long flight prior to your Tanjong Jara holiday, an extremely therapeutic ritual, guaranteed to ease you gently into your new environment, is the *jari-jemari*. Comprising a 10-minute herbal hand-and-foot soak followed by a dynamic massage to improve circulation, reduce inflammation especially in the ankles, relieve numbness and chills in limbs, it's great for under-stretched and over-stressed muscles. Many guests find it offers just the targetted relief needed after having been cooped up in a cramped airline seat for hours.

Another treat to savour takes its inspiration from the time-honoured hot pouch therapy of Malay healing. Warmed bundles of herbs, plants, roots and more are applied to sore, sprained or sad bodies to detoxify and heal. With its probable origins in ancient *orang asli* practice, specially selected ingredients are tied tightly in natural batik cotton cloth, steamed for a few minutes, then dipped in medicated herbal oil and applied to the body. On application, the heat induces sweating, thereby helping to bring toxins to the surface of the skin; then, once the pores are fully open, the skin absorbs the properties of the herbs for deep and satisfying healing.

At Spa Village Tanjong Jara, in keeping with local tradition, hot sand is heated in a wok with fenugreek and blackseed (*Nigella sativa*) seeds, then combined with medicated ointment and applied as a pressure massage to certain areas of the body. Used by local mothers when in confinement, the warmth from the pouches and the pain-relieving properties of the herbs are soothing for joint pains and inflammation. It's a wonderful antidote to the rigours of a long journey.

Raising Spirits to Heal: The East Coast Main Puteri

The *main puteri*, a method whereby spirits are raised by a *bomoh* and attendant musicians to cast out evil spirits or disease, is an ancient art practiced on occasion by east-coast *bomoh* or medicine-men. It usually takes place at night and can take up to several hours to complete.

Most *bomoh* are herbalists, men or women with specialist knowledge of local healing plants. In another category altogether is the spirit-raising *bomoh* – a priest-physician who is able to go into a trance and extract evil spirits or disease from his patients. As such, he is regarded as a master of the science of the occult.

These photographs record a *main puteri* or village performance of such a *bomoh* from the east coast of Malaysia. Accompanied by a fiddler on a three-stringed viol and two drummers, he had been employed by the family of a sick woman who had been struck down by some unknown debilitating disease.

The event began with offerings of rice, coconuts and other fruits to propitiate spirits, then proceeded with a long incantation of music and chanting. This was intended to entice a good spirit to enter the *bomoh's* body: at a certain point this was apparently successful, as the *bomoh* became quite frenzied, casting his body in uncoordinated directions and generally acting as if out of his mind. At this juncture, he is regarded as having become an *orang lupa* ("a man who forgets"), in effect a medium possessed by a helpful spirit.

Once successfully possessed, the music and singing stopped, and the *bomoh* – apparently now acting at the direction of the spirit – approached the sick woman and proceeded to suck, or pretend to suck, around her body until he allegedly located the source of the disease. At this point he sucked the woman's toe and then chanted another incantation or spell. This, we were told, was directed at the disease, encouraging it to be cast out. (In other cases, if the person is possessed by a demon, another spell is chanted, this time to force the demon to be exorcised).

The whole event took several hours, and it was often difficult to really ascertain what was happening at certain times. However, numerous witness accounts of such events have been recorded over the years in Malaysia, and there is no doubt that many such spirit-raising *bomoh* are successful in this type of healing. Whether they really do cast out demons or diseases is not within the remit of this book. But it should be noted that they are often highly respected members of their community – and people generally believe that they do.

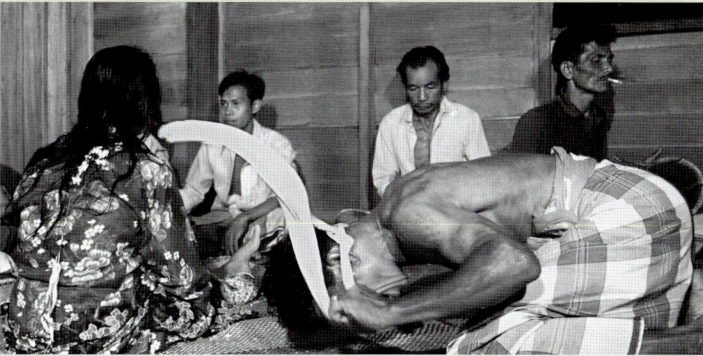

"*Salat* is the ladder leading to proximity (*qurb*) with God."
– Hazrat Khwaja Gharib Nawaz, Sufi saint.

Far left top and bottom Some seated *silat* postures designed to warm up the body; these would usually be done while sitting on a prayer mat after *subuh* prayers in the morning. **Left top** A *silat* posture to regulate breath and stretch the abdomen and lungs. **Left bottom** A balancing *senaman purba* movement designed to promote flexibility and strength.

Another special at Tanjong Jara is the series of Mind, Body, Spirit activities on offer. Based on the bodily movements that Malays from all walks of life (farmers, fisherman, warriors, royalty) have practised to maintain, nourish, revitalise and prolong their lives, it incorporates elements of spiritual *salat* (the internal/external series of exercises Muslims incorporate within their five-times-a-day prayers) and the martial art of *silat*.

Combining several breathing techniques to bring a better sense of clarity and focus with a number of *silat*, *salat* and exercise postures and sequences to enhance endurance and strength, the programme is an uplifting way to bring body and mind back to balance. Facilitated by Captain Mok, the resort's exercise specialist and naturalist, a session begins with some gentle inhalation/exhalation and postures to warm up the body, and is followed by the *senaman purba* yoga-like section that is performed individually or in a moving sequence. It ends with some *silat* standing exercises and a cool-down period that leaves clients centered, grounded and mentally alert.

Above A *silat* posture not unlike a yoga *asana*. A spiritual as well as physical art, *silat* strengthens body and mind. At Tanjong Jara postures with names like *senaman ular* (snake), *senaman harimau* (tiger), *kucing* (cat) and *kuntum* (a bud or woman's private areas) are incorporated into an exercise session in a cool open corridor.

There's no doubt that such exercises have positive mental, physical and emotional effects. Medical research has proven that such disciplined activities encourage the mind to excrete alpha brain waves that create electrical activity leading to altered awareness and deep relaxation. Over time, these manifest themselves in a fitter, toned body as well as an aura of positive health.

It's as the Asians have always said: the inner and the outer are inextricably linked. If a sojourn at Tanjong Jara can achieve improvements in body, mind and soul, the spa and its healing programme is working indeed.

Above and right Dusk is a wonderfully peaceful time at Tanjong Jara, both within the resort (*above*) and at the spa (*right*): subdued lighting, sweet tea lights flickering, starlight and the background symphony of croaking frogs makes for a beguiling atmosphere.

The Past Reborn

SPA VILLAGE MALACCA

Situated in the renovated mansion of a prominent businessman dating from the late 1920s, Spa Village Malacca is the world's first and only spa to base its therapies around the healing culture of the Peranakan people (see overleaf). Part of the Majestic hotel, a classic heritage property in Melaka (Malacca) in the Malaysian peninsula, it is ground-breaking both in treatments and overall wellness strategies.

Truly individual, it's a marvelous mix of Chinese and Malay. There's a facial containing the saliva of swifts from birds' nests highly prized in Chinese cuisine; a scrub that pulls on the potent properties of the local palm sugar or *gula Malacca*; a warming tea served with a spicy *acar* pickle. Fermented

tapioca, chopped guava leaves, fragrant pandan – items more readily found in a *nyonya* wok than a spa stock – are employed in indulgent hair, face and body treatments.

Spa Village has excelled itself here: never before have so many exotic ingredients been used as kitchen cosmetics, and never have they been so artfully presented. Similarly, in-depth research by Malacca-born TCM herbalist, Lee Jok-Keng (see page 121), has revealed many secrets of beauty and wellness practised by Peranakan families. Kept behind closed doors for centuries, these home remedies have found new life with their global premiere at Spa Village Malacca. Intriguing and unusual, they throw insight into a fascinating culture.

Left The airy relaxation lounge, decked out in Peranakan pastels, is the heart of the spa. Large French doors on *right* overlook the pool.

Above Peranakan women prized health and condition of hair as a great beauty asset. This decorative comb would have been used to secure silky tresses.

Peranakan decorative styles included pastel colours, fretwork wood detailing, and bright ceramic tiles – all are employed in the spa rooms and suite.

Left The spacious spa suite, ideal for couples, has a claw-foot tub, shower and toilet as well as massage beds and relaxation corner. With views over the back of the old hotel, it is fresh, convivial and quiet.

AN AUTHENTIC SETTING   It's not only the therapies that are derived from extensive research into local remedies and practices; the setting, too, is authentic with décor reflective of old shophouse architecture and interiors. The Peranakans had a flair for ornamentation, employing gaily painted pastel colours, intricate woodwork, sumptuous furnishings and heavy Victorian furniture in their elaborate homes – and the spa takes its cue from their eclectic tastes.

Elegantly worked in shades of aquamarine and eggshell blue, it is spacious by any standards. The ground floor is given over to a delightful reception and lounging area, along with a series of hair treatment cubicles accessed by *pintu pagar* or saloon-style doors. Floor-to-ceiling windows with louvres and fantail vents invite layered light into a relaxation lounge laid out with traditional Chinese day beds, geometric wall and floor tiles, and delicate fabrics. It's an airy, light space – quiet and secluded for pre- or post-therapy contemplation.

Upstairs, five private treatment rooms and one suite are the epitome of refinement. Custom-crafted wood detailing, porcelain wall tiles, soft batiks in shades of turquoise and kingfisher blue and ornate silverware are easy on the eye; and modern power showers and comfortable massage beds ensure a high level of sophistication. The rich culture of the Peranakans is skillfully evoked in décor, furnishings and form.

The Peranakans

Whilst much is documented about the Chinese, the half-hidden world of the Peranakans is less well known internationally. What is known is that Peranakan, meaning "descendents" or "local-born" depending on who you talk to, is colloquially used to refer to the descendents of the early Chinese community that settled in the Malay and Indonesian archipelagoes around the 17th century. Also known as Baba-Nyonya (*babas* are the males, *nyonyas* the females) they are typically of mixed parentage, with Chinese males marrying local girls (Chinese women weren't allowed by law to leave mainland China until some time in the 19th century).

Also known as Straits Chinese in Malacca, the Peranakans partially adopted Malay customs in an effort to assimilate into local communities, but also maintained many practices from their Chinese roots. Rising to prominence in the Straits Settlements, they evolved a specific culture that was a unique blend of customs and traditions with traces of Portuguese, Dutch, British, Malay, Indonesian and Chinese influences. This includes their own language, a mix of Bahasa and Hokkien; a highly intricate cuisine; personalised dress (women wore Malay batik sarong topped with a *kebaya* or cotton-and-lace figure-hugging blouse, while *babas* favoured Western dress); highly individual forms of interior design and architecture, with a penchant for ornate Victoriana; and specific rituals and ceremonies taken from mainly Taoist and Buddhist sources.

The 12-day wedding ceremony was the most important, but Peranakans still celebrate festivals like Chinese New Year and the Mooncake Festival on a large scale. The older generation continued to observe Chinese religious beliefs and rituals, though many younger Straits Chinese eventually converted to Christianity.

Above Families favoured formal portraiture to document important events. **Below** Art, architecture and food are all highly intricate and individual. *From left*, the facade of the Majestic hotel, detailed work on a shophouse, Peranakan *kueh* or dessert, Malaccan temple.

In Malacca, many Peranakans were traders, merchants or businessmen of one sort or another. They became very influential and often amassed large fortunes, building ornate homes to showcase their wealth. The Majestic Malacca was the home of one such businessman: completed in 1929 as a private mansion, with an architectural style that mirrors Malacca's multi-faceted colonial past, it was sold and converted into a hotel in 1953. The hotel closed down in 2000 and restoration works on the Majestic Malacca took place in 2006. It opened in 2008, this time with a modern accommodation block behind.

Left Some of the key ingredients in Spa Village Malacca's pre-treatment hair ritual: a floral tonic, combs and the zesty lime and flower rinse.

HAIR RITUAL TO BLISS   Inspired by one of the rituals in the elaborate 12-day Peranakan wedding ceremony, every spa guest enjoys a pre-treatment procedure that revolves around the hair. Brides of the past were subjected to a hair cleanse, scalp massage and gentle combing in the open courtyard of her home. This was believed to eradicate impurities and negativity from the girl and bestow good luck on the couple's union.

In the spa, guests are firstly bathed in floral water to dispel negativity, then given a shampoo, comb and scalp massage with virgin olive oil and conditioner. Whilst lying on the custom-crafted recliner and enjoying the pampering, they are able to watch black-and-white movies on a screen embedded into the ceiling. This is an inspired addition, as the focus is on clips from the oeuvre of P Ramlee, Malaysia's cinema legend.

The combination of old-world glamour, period costumes and farcical plots, seen by millions during Malaysia's golden age of cinema, and the soothing hands of the therapist, is an intuitive one. On a physical level, the washing and combing removes dead hair and unblocks hair follicles while the massage improves blood circulation and releases tension in the scalp. On a mental level, stress subsides and the mind wanders back to the 1950s and '60s when life seemed more carefree and innocent. The finale, consisting of a fresh zingy lime and floral rinse, is invigorating and beautifully scented.

A number of treatments, rinses, lotions, infusions and pastes for beautifying, strengthening and improving the health of hair exist in Peranakan archives, emphasising how hair was seen as an integral part of beauty.

Right Lustrous, thick and shiny hair was a sign of *nyonya* beauty, so the Peranakans have a rich culture of hair treatments. Spa Village Malacca offers a warming pandan and coconut hair mask (*top photos and bottom left*) that was traditionally used to give relief from mild headaches and a cooling *limau kasturi* and yoghurt mask using calamansi lime and yoghurt. Both of these are completed with a relaxing scalp massage: Using a mix of acupressure and gentle manipulation, the scalp is squeezed, rubbed and tapped and hair may be combed or pulled. The photo on *bottom right* shows the pre-treatment hair ritual.

The Peranakan bride was prepared for her wedding with a series of cleansing, purifying, skin and hair care rituals.

THE 12-DAY WEDDING CEREMONY   Other aspects of the Peranakan wedding ceremony are integrated into both hotel and spa. Although influenced by Malay customs, festivities and ceremonies were essentially Chinese – and this is evident at Majestic Malacca. Derived from the wedding traditions practised up to the late 19th century in Fujian province in southern China, both brides and grooms were involved in a series of events that gave respect to each other's families, and also prepared the couple for a successful marriage ahead.

In addition to the hair ritual, a bride was expected to bead and embroider a pair of slippers as a present for her fiancée; and the groom's family were obliged to give lavish gifts of clothes and jewellery to stock the bride's trousseau. One of the more symbolic practices included placing a comb of *pisang raja* (a type of banana), a stick of lemongrass and some yam along with three lit incense sticks in an earthenware pot beneath the bridal bed. This was supposed to bring wealth, longevity and fertility to the couple. Another custom called the *an chng* ceremony included the page boy rolling three times over the marriage bed as a blessing for a male first-born child.

Although they were embedded in cultural tradition, these ceremonies had a practical aspect too. Lemongrass and incense sticks keep mosquitoes at bay and yam is often used as a folk remedy for impotence.

The giving and receiving of food and the attendance at elaborate wedding banquets were also highly important, with auspicious dates and times chosen for specific meals. The Peranakan kitchen was called the *perut rumah* or "stomach of the house"; the seat of feminine power, it was the centre of a household's life and activity. It also produced a highly complex cuisine that combines Malay, Chinese and Indian influences to produce a number of spicy, tangy, herbal and sweet dishes.

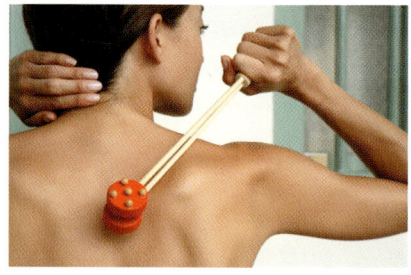

Above A young Peranakan bride in an elebarote jewelled headdress; this was usually an heirloom from the groom's family. **Left** Pre-wedding rituals included cleansing, purifying and massage.

Left Lee Jok-Keng, a TCM herbalist who hails from Malacca, explains the significance of some of the herbs he regularly uses in prescriptions. In TCM, every remedy is tailor-made for individual patients.

Below A selection of herbs regularly used by Jok-Keng in some of the more common prescriptions. Over the centuries remedies have been adapted and changed in TCM, according to new research and development.

Portrait of a Healer: A Chinese Herbalist

Malaccan-born TCM herbalist, Lee Jok-Keng, the person behind Spa Village's Peranakan treatments both in Malacca and Kuala Lumpur, has had an interest in healing since his childhood days. Coming from a devout Buddhist family that spent much of its time caring for both people and animals ("my house was like a zoo, especially with birds and dogs" he jokes), it seemed almost inevitable that Jok-Keng would end up being a doctor.

"We had a close family friend that was an elder Daoist shaman," he recollects, "By the age of 10, I was helping him and hanging out at his place after school. After a couple of years, I became more 'useful' by buying his prescribed herbs for his clients and learning the trade. I also harvested herbs for him in nearby woods and talked to Indians and Malays to get sources and supplies. I massaged his clients and gave instructions to patients when he was out of town."

Jok-Keng recalls eavesdropping on his consultations, putting his ears to the walls to hear his wisdom, and constantly trying to learn more. By the age of 15, in the late 1970s, he had become a full apprentice. "In traditional apprenticeship, you don't get involved with only your field of study, but also with the whole family," he explains. "For me, I tutored his daughters in English, cleaned his ink-brushes and ashtray, went to the wet market and accompanied him for his afternoon coffee, activities all seemingly unrelated to Chinese medicine."

However, he did get to absorb a great deal, even being allowed to hand-copy some of his master's classic texts, a

significant part in the Chinese shamanistic apprenticeship. Further studies followed in the US followed with Jok-Keng graduating in the late 1980s with a major in psychology and a diploma from the National Commission for the Accreditation of Oriental Medicine allowing him to practice TCM in the USA. It was only a matter to time before he returned home to Malaysia to set up his TCM practice in Kuala Lumpur.

Jok-Keng is a firm believer that today's spas can help carry the mantle of traditional healing forms, saying that true healing rituals cannot be separated from the cultural fabric from which they emerged. He is enthusiastic about Spa Village work and has thoroughly enjoyed delving deep into Peranakan culture to create such unusual treatments.

"The processes that go into preparing spa rituals and treatments are as important, if not more important, than the products themselves," he declares.

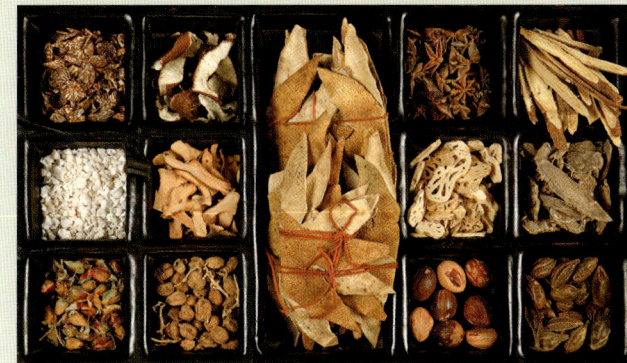

Spa Village Malacca's service with warming and cooling treatments is echoed in the cuisine at the hotel itself: hot and spicy, cool and light.

Left Famous in Asia, but less well known to other cultures, the flavours of Peranakan cuisine are highly individual. Some dishes, specific to Malacca, also borrow freely from Dutch and Portuguese cuisines, reflecting the rich mélange of cultures that have contributed to this town's fascinating history. *Clockwise from top left*: The warm-energy *kerabu* *udang* is a prawn salad flavoured with lemongrass, cucumber, pineapple and spicy chilli. Chinese tea and *acar*, a spicy vegetable pickle commonly served as a condiment, is given at the spa for post-treatment relaxation. A cool-energy, light and not too spicy dish known as *pie tee* comprises small crispy pastry cups filled with sliced turnips and prawns.

YIN AND YANG   Based on the Chinese belief that true wellbeing is the product of a healthy balance of *yin* and *yang* (dark and light, cold and hot), certain foods are thought to have *yin* or cooling properties, while others have warm, *yang* properties. *Nyonya* cuisine aimed for a balance in most dishes, but specifically warm or cool recipes were also followed if necessary. For example, if a person suffered from heartburn due to the consumption of too many spicy, *yang* foods, a doctor would likely prescribe a cool herbal tea to restore the *yin* forces. Similarly, a bout of the flu would be treated with a cooling diet.

At the Majestic, to augment the benefits of the spa, a panel of Peranakan culinary experts has perfected a number of *nyonya* specialties using this hot/cold thesis. A menu of "cool energy" and "warm energy" dishes using local produce and typical Peranakan herbs and spices is an innovative idea at the hotel. Served at lunch in the downstairs lounge or library, and in the more formal upstairs restaurant in the evenings, they're a wonderful introduction to the intricacies of *nyonya* cuisine. They may not be *kueh ee*, the special food prepared for wedding rituals, but they are highly individual nonetheless.

Left The Peranakans were great followers of Victorian fashion, and this three-tiered cake dish would have been a familiar item in any home. Here, at the Majestic, it is used for afternoon tea in the library.

Left, clockwise from top left Eggs for the egg-rolling therapy, whereby hard-boiled eggs are rolled over the body to extract stress, heat and cramping. The treatment is followed with a Thai-style massage. Ingredients in the delicious Malacca palm-sugar and honey body scrub include mineral-rich, grainy sugar and honey, rich in vitamins. Another scrub is composed from guava leaves and yoghurt: cleaning the body of impurities, it's fresh and uplifting, as well as having a wonderful fragrant scent. Ingredients for a nutmeg and rice rolling massage, based on a traditional treatment to remove "wind" from the body. **Opposite** The small pool is a picture of cool and calm.

COOLING AND HEATING TREATMENTS

This *yin/yang* approach is also followed at the spa itself with many foodstuffs found in a typical *nyonya* kitchen cupboard employed in the various treatments on offer. Key culinary ingredients include coconut milk, rice, galangal, ginger, candlenuts, pandan leaves, tamarind juice, lemongrass and fragrant Kaffir lime leaf, all of which are used in one form or another at the spa. These are combined with some delightful treatments based on the home remedies used in Peranakan households.

For example, many Chinese children remember their mothers rolling hard-boiled eggs on bruises; at Spa Village Malacca, a unique body treatment using eggs for "rolling" makes its world-wide spa premiere. Believed to settle hyperactivity, draw out excess heat and help with cramping and swelling, hard-boiled eggs are here employed in a muslin bag and massaged over the body.

After a soothing, hypnotic and, ultimately, healing treatment in the spa, the cool blue pool and comfortable, modernist loungers beckon . . .

Domestic rituals in the *nyonya* domain included facials using a jade roller – cooling, muscle tightening and soothing, the jade roller has been used in ancient China for centuries.

Left Depending on whether the client's body type is warm or cool, the bird's nest facial is given with a warming fermented tapioca mask or a cooling starfruit mask. The main ingredient in the cleanser and moisturiser is the swift spittle (*see right*), while the scrub is composed of sandalwood and watermelon, the toner from liquourice and green tea. The application of the jade roller closes pores and tightens muscles.

On arrival at the spa, guests are asked to fill in a detailed questionnaire that determines whether they are predominantly a cool or warm person. This includes enquiries on health of skin, temperature, digestion and sleep patterns, the answers to which allow the therapist to ascertain whether the client would benefit most from a warming or cooling experience. After diagnosis, in line with Traditional Chinese Medicine practice, certain treatments are recommended.

Spa Village Malacca signature rituals are intriguingly named Suam-Suam Panas Experience and Shiok-Shiok Sejuk Experience. Roughly translating from Bahasa as Warming Heat Treatment and Cool Cold Experience respectively, they each involve a highly unusual sequence that takes its base from *nyonya/baba* traditions along with a hefty dose of TCM.

A cool-energy person would be recommended a Malacca palm sugar and honey scrub, a hot nutmeg and rice rolling body massage, a pandan leaf and coconut milk hair mask and a unique facial that takes bird's nest saliva as its main ingredient. This is combined with the miraculously cool jade roller and a

mask made from fermented tapioca. The warm-energy person, on the other hand, would be encouraged to balance with a body scrub made from yoghurt and chopped guava leaves (high in natural antibiotic properties), an egg rolling body therapy, a calamansi lime and yoghurt hair mask and the same facial, but with the mask made from fresh starfruit. Starfruit is vitamin rich and highly prized in Peranakan culture: lying back with slices of cleansing, cooling starfruit doing their magic on your face is undeniably exotic.

For those who don't have the time or inclination to try the Peranakan specials, there is a short menu of additional therapies that includes some massages and Spa Village signatures such as the *campur-campur* herbal heat pouch treatment and the *lapis-lapis* herbal wrap.

One of the spa's highlights, however, is the comfy lounge; freshly decorated in soothing pastel tones, it makes for a refreshing antidote to Malacca's busy streets. Simply relaxing there with a pot of tea and a magazine between therapies is quietly rejuvenating.

A Traditional Tonic

A luxury ingredient that used to be reserved for special occasions in Chinese households is birds' nest soup, a clear consommé. Containing nests made from the dried spittle of cave-dwelling swifts of the *Collocalia* species, the attraction of the dish is its remedial and restorative tonic value and the knowledge that it is a rare and expensive commodity.

Taking the logic that if something is good for the body it is good for the skin too, such birds' nests are increasingly finding their way into skincare products and therapies. Believed to boost the immune system and bolster longevity, they are now commercially available from farmed swiftlet communities. As such, they are more affordable, but their efficacious anti-aging properties are still intact.

The facial offered at Spa Village Malacca taps into this "caviar of the East" by including the swifts' dried saliva in the cleanser and moisturiser sections of the signature facial. Excellent for dry complexions as it replenishes facial nutrients and improves micro-circulation, it has both rejuvenating and skin softening properties as well. Nobody really knows how the spittle works, but it is very likely that water soluble glycoproteins and monosaccarides or sugars contained in the spittle are the active compounds here. As the specific profile of the active compounds is still vague, scientists simply call them epidermal growth factors (EGFs).

One of the more exotic offerings from Spa Village, the facial has proved a popular option at Malacca. It is a good example of the way in which treatments honour local traditions all the while providing an inventive, sophisticated solution to modern-day ailments.

Even though swifts' nests are now farmed, in the past they were obtained from a breed of swallows found along the coasts of southern China and South East Asia. Their collection was a precarious business with workers climbing up shaky rattan ladders dangling from the ceiling of caves and inching along bamboo ladders to gather the nests. As many were some 60 m (200 ft) above sea level, the risks were considerable.

Bringing to life the glorious past of the Peranakans, the Majestic Malacca is a prime example of restoration for re-use. Sensitivity to site permeates throughout.

THE HISTORY LIVES ON In many ways, Spa Village Malacca (and the hotel itself) reflects Malacca's multi-faceted past. A town with a strong colonial heritage – at one time or another it has been ruled by the Dutch, the Portuguese and the British – and plenty of Chinese, Malay and Indian influences, it is rich in history and culture. From the heady days of the 15th-century Malacca Sultanate, through its heyday as one of the important trading posts of the Straits Settlements, to today's multi-cultural town, Malacca is unique.

A stay at this classic hotel, where authentic decor produces an atmosphere in keeping with its history, is both rewarding and educational. The hotel is proud to commemorate its place at the centre of the local community and sees itself – and its unique spa – as a flagship for the region.

Keeping age-old traditions alive with innovative offerings is Spa Village's forte, and Majestic Malacca more than honours this reputation. The empires may have fallen in this ancient outpost, but the history lives on.

Opposite left The forecourt of the gracious Majestic hotel is home to an ancient bonsai tree. The new accommodation block is just visible behind. **Opposite right** A sensitive restoration job on the old mansion has resulted in a heritage hotel in shades of aqua and eggshell blue. The lobby lounge is a purist's dream: original floor tiles newly agleam mix with heavy period furniture and furnishings. **Left** A small pool sited between the new block and the old building has comfy loungers, perfect for post-spa respite.

A Balinese Village Experience

SPA VILLAGE RESORT TEMBOK, BALI

Ask a question about Bali, and people tend to gush. "The people are so gentle and kind, genuinely hospitable" . . . " The landscape, with undulating rice fields and emerald green hues, is timeless" . . . "There is an inherent spirituality permeating throughout" . . . "The culture is still so alive today!" . . . and more – much more – in the same vein.

Cliché or not, there is more than a grain of truth in the above sentiments. Inclusively and universally, people seem to react to Bali in a positive manner. It's as if the island has the spooky ability of casting a spell over its visitors, drawing and luring them into its embrace. And before they know it, they've

fallen in love with the place: they want to learn more about the island, its ancient culture, its spirituality, its healing rituals, its magic and mores, its art and architecture and its remarkably resilient people.

This is where Spa Village Resort Tembok comes in: A destination spa situated in a calm and reclusive environment on Bali's north east coast. With its out-of-the-way, illuminating environment and authentic personal wellness programmes, it is the ideal place in which to immerse body and soul in the real, untouched and pure spirit of Bali. It isn't surprising that many visitors have reported life changing experiences here.

Left The tranquil pool, with attendant *balés* and loungers, is at the heart of the resort. A magnet for seclusion seekers, it is also serviced by a lady serving *jamu* (seen in background).

Above Yoga, taught by a Balinese dancer, is part of the Balance programme at the resort. Morning sessions are a spiritually uplifting way to start the day and bespoke sessions are also available.

To the Balinese, spirituality is as vital as breathing: It takes the form of Hinduism merged with an ancient belief in the spirits of the natural world.

This page and opposite Sometimes called the Island of a Thousand Temples, Bali actually has more than 20,000 temples, as well as an infinite number of house-hold temples. Be they village temples, *kawitan* temples devoted to village ancestors, *melanting* temples in the markets, *subak* irrigation temples, temples on beaches, lakes, mountains, rivers and more, they are very much living entities patronised by most of the population. People visit to give thanks, pay their respects, make requests and celebrate. In addition, offerings are given daily to shrines in the family compound. This humility and respect for elders and the divine permeates throughout all of Balinese life – even in the spa.

SPIRITUAL, MENTAL, PHYSICAL AND EMOTIONAL BALANCE

To try to explain Bali's spirituality is outside the confines of this book, but suffice it to say that its all-pervading presence dictates much of Balinese day-to-day existence. On a macrocosmic level there are gods, mortals and demons. Physically, there are heads, torsos and feet; there is birth, life and death. The highest is the first, the lowest the last. Even on a language level, there is high or refined Balinese for speaking to priests, medium Balinese for strangers and people of higher caste, and low or common Balinese reserved for friends and family. Order and rules relate to both spiritual and physical matters and to the universe as a whole.

This outlook, characterised as it is by threes, is mirrored in the physical landscape: Mount Agung, the mighty 3,142-metre-high (10,300 feet) sacred volcano in the eastern central part of the island, is the abode of the gods; the surrounding island is the home of people; the sea, full of demons, is to be avoided, distrusted and feared. In every village, there are temples, houses and animal pens.

In order to keep the delicate balance of this tri-partite Balinese world, gods need to be worshipped and spirits placated. Around this has grown a huge number of ceremonies, rituals and rites of passage that are conducted daily or at auspicious dates in one's lifetime. As there is no distinction

between the spiritual and the secular, the outer and the inner, they are all designed to keep evil forces at bay and good ones content. Be it in the presenting of the *canang*, the everyday offering set on a tray made of woven young coconut leaves, the fashioning of an artwork, or the conducting of a deeper ritual, all acts are done with grace, submissiveness and an earnest desire that all should be well.

At Spa Village Resort Tembok, Bali's essence is evoked in a number of wellness programmes that have been formulated to honour the deep-seated culture of the island. With healing – spiritual, mental, physical and emotional – at their heart, they are based on these traditional Balinese beliefs and practices.

Bali's devotional spirituality can be found in prayer, music, dance, song, painting, carving, yoga, and more.

THREE PATHS TO WELLNESS

Falling under three broad categories – Balance, Creativity and Vigour – there are three Discovery Paths to wellness at Spa Village Resort Tembok. Offered both separately and incorporating elements from each other's, programmes are tailor made to suit the personal goals of the client. Whether the ultimate aim is relaxation, recovery, self-discovery or rejuvenation, the guest's journey is carefully monitored throughout.

On arrival at the resort, guests are questioned about their needs and wants. A spa coordinator discusses the various options on offer, giving advice as to which pursuits best match the client's objectives. The emphasis is on seclusion and reflection along with elements of the island's ancient healing culture.

The Balance programme includes such activities as yoga, beach walking, after-dark starlight gazing while floating in the

Above left Yoga's benefits are many: On a physical level, practitioners report increased flexibility, better lubrication of joints, toned muscles and detoxification. These are joined by spiritual and mental benefits as well, so it is the ideal practice for those on a self-discovery path at the resort.
Above Every Balinese is adept at weaving offering baskets; guests are also taught this simple art to participate in island culture.

pool (see opposite) and cruising at sunset. Creativity, as the name suggests, includes *lontar* and wood carving, painting and weaving instruction (see above), as well as outings to Balinese dance or musical performances. Vigour tends to lean towards the physical with lessons in the martial art of *pencak silat* (see pages 146–147), participation in the fitness circuit, swimming, snorkeling and diving. These may be inter-mixed at will and all incorporate some innovative spa treatments as well.

Meditation with Flotation

A very special experience to be had at Spa Village Resort Tembok is the hypnotic Starlight Gazing Meditation session, where the client lies weightless on a floating platform in the pool listening to a very particular soundtrack of music and taking in the enormity of the universe above. An innovative addition to any spa menu, it is another of the "firsts" that Spa Village is so famous for.

The music is designed to induce deep relaxation, while coaxing the brain into a "synchronised theta state of consciousness". A combination of chimes, bells, chants, hums and electronic vibrations, it is believed to help expand consciousness and encourages the recipient to open heart and mind.

While floating on the pool, taking in the night sky, palm fronds and stars above, the music literally transports you: you'll find the mind opening, the body naturally relaxing, heartbeat slowing, muscles easing out and respiration becoming more regular and slow. The feeling of weightlessness and the view of the infinite night sky are a powerful combination.

It's a wonderful opportunity to totally "let go", allow thoughts to enter the mind and flow out again, to review emotions and contemplate deep within. Incorporating a couple of sessions into a week-long retreat reinforces the resort's aim of helping clients on a path to self-discovery, wellness and peace.

On arrival, after a fairly lengthy drive from the airport through Bali's magical hinterland, the combination of low-key atmosphere, understated luxury and caring staff is most welcoming. Guests are seated in an airy reception pavilion for registration – and given their first treat: A foot bath and gentle foot exfoliation with crushed volcanic stone and a sublime neck and head massage. The Balinese believe that when they leave home their feet may pick up some of the earth's plentiful bad spirits, so this foot bath and scrub not only cleanses physically, it washes away potential pollution as well. Many guests comment that the ritual sets the tone for the whole experience that is to follow.

Afterwards, guests are free to explore the intimate retreat, further relax and refresh, and plan their activities. With only 27 rooms, two suites and two stand-alone villas, accommodations combine Balinese elements (fabrics, carved timber motifs) with modern comfort and luxury. The garden, with frangipani, bougainvillea and midnight blue infinity-edge pool is cool and quiet, while supremely restful *balés* and loungers provide comfort. A variety of nutritious meals, snacks and juices (see page 145) are served in a large open-sided *wantilan* restaurant by the ocean. And, of course, there is the spa with its carefully selected menu of Balinese-inspired treatments.

Opposite far left After a two- or three-hour drive to the resort, the welcoming foot bath and head and neck massage provides sweet relief. A refreshing thirst quencher that flushes kidneys and reduces heat is also offered on arrival.

Opposite right top and right Balinese healing culture is honoured in the spa suites, where local flowers, fabrics and artifacts are tastefully displayed.

Opposite right bottom The row of spa suites is differentiated from the other rooms by soft drapes outside and a verandah where *jamu* is served after every treatment.

Overleaf The pool is the resort's magnet; sandwiched between sea and garden, it is cool and inviting.

Honouring Balinese healing culture is a priority in every aspect of the resort – in treatments, food, drink, daily routine, décor and more.

Left Packed with steamed lemongrass and pandan leaves, warmed bundles of magic are pressed along the body in the Spa Village signature *campur-campur* treatment offerd at most of the group's spas.

TRADITIONAL TREATMENTS FROM BALI

In keeping with Spa Village's philosophy of offering authentic treatments, the spa menu is based on effective Balinese remedies that have been around for centuries. As with other Asian cultures, many villagers are knowledgeable about herbal medicine, often growing a small garden of medicinal herbs (an *apotek hidup* or "living pharmacy") in their family compound.

Mainly made from leaves, barks, roots and seeds, the prescriptions take two forms: internal and external. For internal use, the substances are boiled in water and the resulting infusion or *loloh* is drunk. For external use, ingredients are pounded or mashed and the mix or *boreh* is smeared on the body. Some are designed to cool the body, others to heat it up. If there is an excess of "wind" and the patient is chilled or fluey, a preparation with a hot substance such as ginger or clove is used; if the patient has what is known as a "hot stomach", something cold such as cucumber is applied.

Spa Village Resort Tembok, Bali offers some variations on these age-old remedies. One particular ritual, the *penganten melukat* signature experience, based on the cleansing treatments

couples undergo before their wedding day, incorporates a massage, *boreh* body scrub using a mix of pounded cloves, ginger, galangal, turmeric and rice, a milk cleanse and a flower bath. With its powerful clove scent, the *boreh* can be quite steamy, not to mention skin exfoliating and deeply heating in the muscles. In Balinese families, the scrub is usually administered by the bride and groom's mother or grandmother; then, after the wedding, the couple are blessed by the priest with holy water at the temple. This recreated treatment is much more than a symbol of letting go of the old and embracing the new.

Above left The resort's traditional Balinese facial or *mesipat* is heaven sent. Seen here are the scrub and mask; the latter is taken from a local recipe that is used to clear bruises as it works on the circulation. **Above right and right** A time-honoured Balinese treatment, the nutmeg *boreh* is known for its heating properties. It is used to relieve muscle aches.

Left and below Poorly nourished hair is literally fed with goodness from local market ingredients in the *mekramas* or hair conditioning treatment. Based on a rural remedy, it relies on hibiscus leaves (used before the advent of shampoo in Bali as the mashed leaves excrete a cleansing sticky gel), candlenuts for their high oil content (to make hair glossy) and coconut oil for moisturising. In Bali, grandmothers still wash their hair in coconut milk: thick milk is used to wash and massage while younger coconut milk is reserved for conditioning and rinsing.

Other herbaceous treatments include the *mekramas*, a hair conditioning treatment that uses a paste of fresh aloe gel pounded with hibiscus leaves and a head massage given with coconut oil, candlenuts, hibiscus leaves and aloe vera, as well as a traditional facial or *mesipat*. In the latter, the toner is made from a cooling juice of pressed cucumber, the scrub is a potent combo of finger-root, crushed rice and turmeric, the mask comprises pure sandalwood and the massage is conducted with soothing lime and honey. Between each section, the face is wiped clean and refreshed with a wonderful scented, hot towel.

Each treatment is preceded by the Spa Village Resort Tembok, Bali's signature steam-and-sand treat and culminates with a locally brewed *jamu* drink (see page 145). The former is conducted in a specially designed semi-open room (see opposite) where a pit of volcanic sand beneath a bamboo lid is combined with a steam. While your toes curl into a bed of very cool soft sand, the legs are steamed until they feel quite sweaty. A cold towel on the neck keeps the temperature down, while the sand between the toes exfoliates. During this hot/cold sensation, you can luxuriate with an *es bola*, a shaved ice and palm sugar confection, a traditional Balinese delicacy, before splashing in the attendant waterfall to wash off the sand.

It's a real delight – indulgent, playful and soothing – and sets the client up for the deeper therapy to follow.

Above and left Spa Village Resort Tembok, Bali utilises its locale in an imaginative way with its signature pre-treatment ritual called the *segara giri*. A homage to its unique location, *segara* translates as "ocean" and *giri* as "mountain". Based on the principle that governs saunas and steams, it gives a simultaneous heating and cooling sensation along with black sand exfoliation on the feet. A traditional tonic ends the ritual.

Volcanic Sand Magic

Clays, muds, sand and stones – once considered everyday and humdrum – are now seen as precious resources in the spa world. Prized for their detoxifying, exfoliating and cleansing properties, they have the ability to relieve aches and pains, draw out impurities and give a healthy, shining glow to once-tired skin.

As Spa Village Resort Tembok, Bali is located between the island's most sacred volcano and the Lombok straits, the beach comprises a long narrow strip of black volcanic sand. Formed by lava flowing into the ocean, it is rich in minerals. In fact, the Balinese regularly bury themselves in the beach, believing that the hot sand cures a myriad of diseases from skin conditions to arthritis and back pain. Certainly, the moisturising effect and high mineral content would help with skin problems and ailments such as fungal infections.

Sand has the ability to retain its temperature for a long time, so when applied hot, it is useful for joint conditions and to reduce water retention, and when applied cold, can be beneficial on the skin's surface. At the spa it comprises part of the signature sand-and-steam treatment whereby cool sand underfoot exfoliates and re-mineralises skin and hot steam above increases blood circulation, draws out toxins and prepares skin for the treatment that follows.

It's a wonderfully indulgent treat – especially as it is given in a private indoor-outdoor salon where intricately carved Balinese statuary, the sound of water and sea breezes are your only companions.

Knowing as we do the benefits, it's only a matter of time before sand wraps, hot pouches filled with sand and herbs, mud masks and an all-over sand bath will be offered at the spa.

Jamu and Juices: Refreshing Naturally

"We are what we eat", so the adage goes, but in Indonesia the expression "we are what we drink" may be more apt. Many Indonesians of all ages, classes and ethnicities regularly drink a glass of *jamu* daily. A herbal beverage, made from plants, roots, barks, leaves, honey, fruits and more, a *jamu* drink is more than a mere tonic. It's a revitaliser, a strengthener, a beauty aid and a health-giver. It may also be taken for kidney disease, impotence, whitening of the skin – and a host of other ills.

Jamu's origins are difficult to trace, as its production (as with many village healing traditions) is not well documented. Rather, *jamu* recipes have traditionally been handed down orally from mother to daughter and production tends to be of the cottage industry type. Different *jamu* are made by different villages and families. What is known, however, is that there are more than 350 different *jamu* drinks regularly made and drunk across the Indonesian archipelago – and hundreds of thousands of people swear to their efficacy.

Most common *jamu* contain turmeric for its astringent qualities, tamarind for blood cleansing and ginger for flavouring and aiding digestion. Other gingers, such as galangal and the resurrection lily rhizome, are regularly used as are a host of spices such as cinnamon, nutmeg, mace, cloves, fennel, black and white pepper, cardamom, coriander, cumin and caraway seeds.

Spa Village Resort Tembok, Bali's *jamu* lady from one of the local villages visits the resort twice daily carrying her *jamu* bottles, as is traditional in Bali, in a basket on her head. While you may find the taste a little unusual, it can gradually grow on you. The addition of honey is often offered to sweeten the bitter flavour.

As an alternative, an Australian herbalist has devised a number of health-giving juices and smoothies: made from fresh and exotic fruits, they are rich in minerals, vitamins, enzymes, fibre and phyto-nutrients (agents of rejuvenation). Flavourings have a distinctly Balinese feel, with wild Balinese cacao, vanilla bean, cinnamon, ginger and lime used liberally. There are a variety of blends useful for the digestion, relaxation, invigoration, balance and more. They'll flush out toxins, rehydrate organs, increase blood circulation and give you an energy boost.

With its roots in ancient Chinese Shaolin monasteries, *pencak silat* combines movement, breath and energy techniques to create a powerful martial art.

Opposite and right

Although it isn't really known how this defensive martial art reached Bali's shores, it is believed to have been introduced to the island from Java and is now widely practised. Called *pencak silat*, it differs from other *silat* forms in a number of ways as, once intertwined with Balinese culture, new moves and techniques were created. At Spa Village Resort Tembok, Bali, *pencak silat* classes are given to guests by a local expert, who learnt the art from his uncle some 100 metres distance from the hotel. Using high and low moves and open and closed guards, it involves fast, strong and powerful punching and kicking as well as some graceful steps and sequences. Arm and body movements resemble some Balinese dance moves, as do the eloquent facial expressions characterised by glinting eyes. A session on the beach is guaranteed to raise the metabolism and uplift the mind: some would argue it is a form of physical meditation.

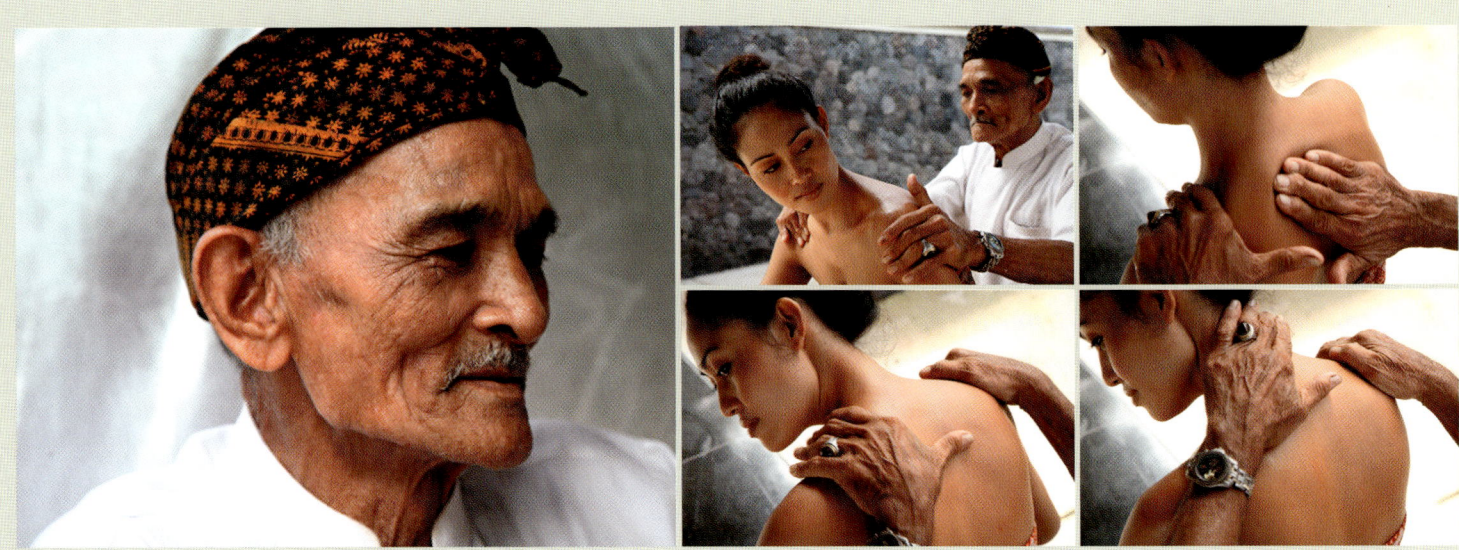

Portrait of a Healer: A Balinese Masseur

The word *balian* is often translated as "witch doctor" or "traditional healer", but is, in fact, a shaman. Blessed with spiritual powers, such people have the ability to enter what the Balinese call the mystical world and commune with spirits. Nonetheless, *balians* are also healers, acting as spirit mediums, prophesisers, casters of spells, interpreters of various phenomena and masseuses. There are many different types, and a village usually houses at least one *balian*.

Even though there are general practitioners in Bali, villagers are just as likely, possibly more likely, to seek the services of a *balian* rather than a doctor. The Balinese believe that ill health, an accident or crop failure are not simply the result of bad luck. They are directly caused by the supernatural, so family members immediately present offerings to both gods and demons to try to reverse the damage.

If this does not work, they may try to atone themselves or their bad actions that caused the misfortune in the first place by consulting a traditional healer or *balian*. Amongst others, there is the *balian manak* or midwife; the *balian tulang* or bonesetter; and the *balian apun* or masseur. The latter should not be confused with an ordinary masseur: Although they are in possession of physical massage skills, such *balians* are also able to heal through "magic", by giving offerings, chanting spells, seeking divine intervention or by some other mystical means.

It is believed that *balians* receive their special powers through different sources. Some are able to go into a trance, others have inherited their skills from family members, yet others have served an apprenticeship from another *balian*. Some are illiterate, while others are learned, skilled at reading *lontars* or palm leaf manuscripts inscribed with age-old remedies in ancient Balinese. All fall under the broad umbrella term of "healer".

One example of a traditional healer (though not a shaman) is Kak Nyoman Tis (*kak* means grandfather), a 75-year-old man who lives locally to Spa Village Resort Tembok, Bali. When he was a boy, Kak Tis observed his grandfather giving massages, but didn't actually start practising himself until he was about 70. He says he suddenly felt the calling to do so – and found that he had inherited the powers of his ancestors.

People come to him if they have any aches and pains, illness or problems that they cannot solve. With the aid of a small piece of wood (which he found in his family shrine) he can ascertain if the problem is simply physical or the result of spirits' actions. He is then able to modify his massage techniques accordingly.

If the problem is the result of something non-physical, he uses his palm to literally push the problem out of the body. If it is something rheumatic or arthritic, he'll use long strokes with palms down going in an upward direction, a technique that is similar to lymphatic massage. If the person is lacking vitality, he concentrates on the armpits, the groin area and the buttocks to increase circulation and rejuvenate and energise the meridians in the body.

All Kak Tis's massage styles are quite dynamic and vigorous; as with "normal" Balinese massage, they are therapeutic in nature, so a session with him is uplifting rather than relaxing. Considering that he had never massaged another person in his life before he reached the age of 70 and has never had any formal training, his massage is quite extraordinary. By concentrating on areas with lymph nodes, he instinctively works on problem areas.

When questioned about his powers, Kak Tis simply smiles and looks heavenward. There's no need for explanation in his mind.

Spirituality is so deep-seated in Bali that people are almost unconsciously living the spa life, with daily meditation, giving to others and healing. The resort seeks to emulate that lifestyle – and, for the most part, succeeds.

Left The resort, with its particular stillness and serenity is an ideal venue to gain insight into oneself.

A PERSONAL JOURNEY   It soon becomes obvious that the focus at Spa Village Resort Tembok, Bali is on personal reflection. To help guests relax and unwind, all is understated, unobtrusive and serene. Against a soundtrack of birdsong, rolling surf and crowing cocks as well as the occasional barking dog, clients have a chance to switch off, participating in as much or as little of the three Discovery Paths' activities as they wish.

For those who are keen to seek a deeper understanding of Balinese culture, a Spa Village Academy is offered. Giving insight into Balinese philosophy, spirituality and healing, there are classes in massage technique by a 75-year-old healer, as well as tuition into the theory of Balinese healing, *lulur* and *jamu* therapy, and the daily spa treatments practiced in the region.

As guests give themself up to the local rhythms of the resort, many report that they are not only absorbing new knowledge, they are learning about themselves too. In fact, self-discovery lies at the heart of this restful retreat. As clients delve into the ancient Balinese way of life, they are guided on a journey that is akin to a pilgrimage. The ultimate aim is to find what is deep within. And, as Bali's strong spirituality is imbued throughout, it shouldn't come as a surprise that repeat guests are becoming the norm.

BALI'S BEAUTY ALL AROUND   Of course it helps
that all this bliss-out is conducted in an environment that is at
once peaceful, beautiful and entirely natural. The nearby village
of Tembok with its fine temple complex is a short walk away, but
the immediate surrounds include only sea, sand, coconut groves
and horizon. With a prime beachfront location and the shadow
of majestic Gunung Agung behind, the resort is a geographic
as well as a spiritual retreat.

RICE: A GIFT FROM GOD

Rice, to the Balinese, is much more than a staple foodstuff. Used in offerings, healing therapies, ceremonies and more, it is an integral part of Bali's cultural life.

The cycle of preparing the paddy fields, then planting, irrigating and harvesting the rice plants, is bound by complex rituals and customs. At certain stages, ceremonies are held and offerings are presented to Dewi Sri, the goddess of rice, in order to maintain the balance of Nature and ensure a good crop. These ceremonial patterns reinforce the traditional *subak* irrigation system – a complex ecosystem of rice paddies based around the local water temple. This system not only provides environmental and agricultural stability ensuring that water levels are maintained in every villager's fields, but also binds people together.

Every day, offerings of rice (examples of such are pictured above) are ceremoniously given in thanks to the gods, and every day, rice is served with every meal. In addition, a few grains of rice always accompany flowers and fruits in home and temple offerings. Rice, pound into powder, is used in many home-made therapies: added to ground coffee beans, it is used as a *kopi* scrub; mixed with ground nutmeg or cloves, it forms the basis for the warming *boreh*; and ground into the finest of powders, it doubles up as a pressed face powder that adds a fine translucent matte appearance to the complexion.

Be it food, fodder, cosmetic or ceremonial, rice plays a special role in the hearts and lives of every resident of Bali. It's a gift from God, the people say.

Opposite From field to fodder, ornamentation to offering, rice is central to Balinese life. Whether a person is making an intricate patterned offering or a replication of Dewi Sri (*bottom photos*), the work is done with love.

Above The mighty profile of Gunung Agung rises up behind the resort. When it comes to planting rice, the corner of the field closest to Gunung Agung is the first to be planted; these same plants are the first to be harvested also.

Spa Village Products

To give clients the chance to replicate the aromas and textures they experienced at the various spas, Spa Village has created a very special selection of products for home use. There's a variety of body and essential oils, aromatic candles and cones, scrubs, soaps and herbal baths, as well as teas and tonics; each and every product is 100 percent natural, using the healing properties and scents of locally grown herbs, plants and flowers.

Based on ancient formulas of Malaysian healing – be it Indian, Chinese and Malay – all the products are totally pure. Whether it is a herbal pillow for a dreamless sleep, a deeply penetrating massage oil, or a whimsical soap-on-a-rope, each is carefully crafted for quality, practicality and longevity. Great as gifts for loved ones or for me-time, Spa Village products are available for purchase at all the resorts and spas. For a preview of some of these gorgeous gifts, see opposite.

Aromatic soaps for relaxing, uplifting or purifying the body are great for all over cleansing.

Relaxing, uplifting or purifying body oils use a range of herbs and florals for deep penetration.

The *minyak* range of traditional Malay oils are multi-purpose medicated oils, great for healing.

Essential oils come in 10ml bottles; they use exotic flowers like ylang-ylang and patchouli.

For those who want to try rattan tapping at home, a set of Chinese sticks is available.

Sodium soap from palm oils, cocamide and essential oils are playfully attached on a rope.

Aroma cones contain a blend of pure essential oil of ylang-ylang, patchouli, grapefruit, cedarwood, rosemary and lavender.

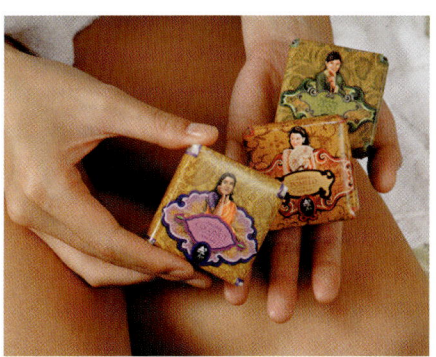

In packs of six, these traditional soaps are made with palm oil, palm kernal, clove, lemon, pomelo, nutmeg, coconut and lemongrass.

The Traditional Malay Range includes a *boros puteri* herbal body scrub and *akar-akar*, an anti-oxidant drink to enhance body vitality.

YTL Hotels & Resorts

**JW MARRIOTT HOTEL
KUALA LUMPUR**
183 Jalan Bukit Bintang,
55100 Kuala Lumpur,
Malaysia.
tel: (603) 2715 9000
fax: (603) 2715 7000
email: jwmkl@ytlhotels.com.my
website: www.ytlhotels.com

**THE RITZ-CARLTON,
KUALA LUMPUR**
168, Jalan Imbi,
55100 Kuala Lumpur,
Malaysia.
tel: (603) 2142 8000
fax: (603) 2711 8143
email: rckl@ytlhotels.com.my
website: www.ritzcarlton.com

PANGKOR LAUT RESORT,
Pangkor Laut Island,
32200 Lumut, Perak,
Malaysia.
tel: (605) 699 1100
fax: (605) 699 1200
email: plr@ytlhotels.com.my
website: www.pangkorlautresort.com

TANJONG JARA RESORT
Batu 8 Off Jalan Dungun
23000 Dungun,
Terengganu,
Malaysia.
tel: (609) 845 1100
fax: (609) 845 1200
email: tjr@ytlhotels.com.my
website: www.tanjongjararesort.com

CAMERON HIGHLANDS RESORT
By The Golf Course
39000 Tanah Rata, Cameron Highlands,
Pahang,
Malaysia.
tel: (605) 491 1100
fax: (605) 491 1800
email: chr@ytlhotels.com.my
website: www.cameronhighlandsresort.com

THE MAJESTIC MALACCA

188 Jalan Bunga Raya,

75100 Melaka,

Malaysia.

tel: (606) 289 8000

fax: (606) 289 8080

email: tmm@ytlhotels.com.my

website: www.majesticmalacca.com

Spa Village Resort Tembok, Bali

Jalan Singaraja-Amlapura No100

Desa Tembok,

Tejakula Buleleng,

Bali,

Indonesia.

tel: (60 3) 2783 1000 (Administration
& Reservation)

fax: (60 3) 2148 7397

email: travelcentre@ytlhotels.com.my

website: www.spavillage.com

VISTANA HOTEL KUALA LUMPUR

9 Jalan Lumut,

Off Jalan Ipoh,

50400 Kuala Lumpur,

Malaysia.

tel: (603) 4042 8000

fax: (603) 4041 1400

email: viskl@ytlhotels.com.my

website: www.vistanahotels.com

VISTANA HOTEL KUANTAN

Jalan Telok Sisek,

25000 Kuantan,

Pahang,

Malaysia.

tel: (609) 517 8000

fax: (609) 517 8400

email: viskn@ytlhotels.com.my

website: www.vistanahotels.com

VISTANA HOTEL PENANG

213 Jalan Bukit Gambir,

Bukit Jambul,

11950 Penang,

Malaysia.

tel: (604) 646 8000

fax: (604) 646 1400

email: vispg@ytlhotels.com.my

website: www.vistanahotels.com

For reservations or enquiries, please
contact:

YTL Travel Centre

tel: (603) 2783 1000

fax: (603) 2148 7397

email: travelcentre@ytlhotels.com.my

Glossary

Abhyangam The term given to the most common form of Ayurvedic massage which is therapeutic, not relaxing. Taken from the root word *ang* meaning "movement" and the prefix *abhi* meaning "into" or "toward", *abhyangam* refers to both the movement of toxins into the alimentary canal for elimination and the moving of energy into the body. It is traditionally performed with a lot of medicated herbal oil chosen according to one's *dosha*, and is performed by one, two, four, or more therapists.

Aromatherapy Treatments (massage, facials and more) that include the application of fragrant essential oils. Different oils have different therapeutic benefits.

Asana Indian term for a posture in yoga.

Ayurveda Ancient Indian medical "Science of Life": complete herbal system for healing that incorporates treatments, diet, lifestyle and more.

Boros Malay word for a particular facial or body scrub that utilises fresh herbal ingredients.

Campur-campur Meaning a "blending of varieties" in Malay, this special Spa Village creation combines massage with the application of steaming hot pouches filled with lemongrass and pandan leaves all over the body. Touch, tone and aromatherapy combine with the best of Thai and Malay massage techniques.

Gu Fang Xun Shen Also known as Ancient Body Smoking, this is a traditional Chinese technique used to rid the body of negative energies. Incense, of which acorus root is the main ingredient, is wafted over the entire body with special focus on several points for a potent cleansing effect.

Hydrotherapy Treatments using water to tone muscles, boost the circulation and more. They vary from hot spring bathing to underwater massage, jets and showers.

Ikal-ikal Malay term for a traditional herbal hair roots treatment that protects the scalp and promotes healthy hair.

Jari-jemari A hand and foot soak in a warm herbal bath, followed by a scrub and massage to soothe and pamper tired limbs.

Lapis-lapis A type of Malay herbal wrap, whereby a mixture of lemongrass, ginger, galangal and camphor is applied to the body, which is then wrapped in warm sheets. It helps to detoxify, reduce water retention and relieve joint and muscle pain.

Lomi-lomi Massage A Polynesian healing treatment incorporating long and broad massage strokes, as well as a rocking motion, to ease muscle pain, promote relaxation and produce an overall sense of wellbeing.

Lulur A Javanese courtly treatment, originally used by royalty to improve skin and muscle tone, the *lulur*'s main ingredient is turmeric. It comprises an exfoliating body scrub, followed by a body splash of fresh yoghurt to nourish and re-moisturise skin. It is often accompanied by a massage at the beginning and a floral bath at the end of the treatment.

Lymphatic Drainage Massage A special type of massage technique where a pumping motion is used to help drain away pockets of water retention and toxins.

Meditation A form of mental discipline, widely practised in the East, that focuses on breath, using a mantra or some other technique to reduce stress and fatigue, but primarily to obtain some connection with the Divine.

Moxabustion Using a lighted herbal stick to heat up various acupoints in the body, this TCM therapy is primarily prescribed for dispelling cold, promoting circulation and activating key points in the body.

Mukha lepam Taken from *mukha* meaning "face" and *lepam* which translates as "pack", this is an Ayurvedic facial treatment that uses herbal pastes and facial massage to condition and nourish skin, open blocked pores, eliminate toxins and cleanse the face, thereby improving overall skin texture.

Onsen   A Japanese hot, usually volcanic, spring bath. Full of minerals, people take to these waters to help with sore or aching muscles, and as a social activity.

Reflexology   A TCM technique that uses pressure point massage on the feet to restore the flow of energy throughout the entire body. Certain points on the feet are believed to coordinate with particular organs or parts of the body.

Rotenburu   An outdoor bath most often made from Japanese cypress, marble or granite that is fed with *onsen* water.

Scrub   An exfoliation process by which the top layer of dead skin cells is sloughed off the face or body, usually with the application of herbals pastes or by dry-brushing.

Silat   Asian form of martial art, practiced in Indonesia and Malaysia, that comprises postures, movements and sequences aligned with breath and meditation.

Sirodhara   One of the best known Ayurvedic therapies, sirodhara comes from *siro* ("head") and *dhara* ("pouring of herbal liquids on specific body parts"). It denotes the continuous pouring of herbal oils, milk, buttermilk or ghee over the head and scalp to heal, balance, relax and eliminate toxins.

Siro lepam   Taken from the Hindi words, *siro* meaning "head" and *lepam* translating as "pack", the treatment is an authentic Indian four-part head, neck, face and shoulder massage along with a head pack to stimulate hair growth and revitalize the brain.

TCM (Traditional Chinese Medicine)
Ancient Chinese system of wellness that incorporates herbal pills and potions, martial art exercises, massage, therapies such as acupressure and acupuncture, and more, with prevention of disease and overall wellness its primary aims.

Tai chi quan   An extensive Chinese martial art system of therapeutic breathing and postural and moving exercises, designed to develop inner stamina and circulate energy in body and mind.

Tui-na an mo Massage
Designed to redirect the flow of *chi* in the body and open up blocked meridians, this traditional massage comes from the Chinese words *tui* (to push) and *na* (to grasp), *an* (to press or push downwards) and *mo* (to rub). Although it takes into consideration the tendo-muscular system, its focus is on influencing the organs at a deeper level for profound healing.

Ukup wangi   Malay term for a traditional scented body steaming with flowers, herbs etc.

Unani   Originating in Greece with the philosopher-physician Hippocrates (460–377 BC), Unani is a traditional form of medicine practised widely in the Moslem world. Unani remedies are usually herbal, although ingredients of animal, marine and mineral origin are used. Humoural theory (the presence and balance of blood, phlegm, yellow bile and black bile) is at its heart.

Wrap   A therapy whereby the body is covered with oils, muds, herbs or a combination thereof, then wrapped in a heat-inducing sheet in order to induce sweating. The properties of the wrap are encouraged through the heat to enter the skin, whilst toxins and impurities are expelled.

Yoga   Ancient Hindu discipline that comprises breathing exercises with focused meditation and a variety of stretching movements and postures. Designed to unite mind, body and spirit, it is a deeply philosophical balancing art.